Why Won't They Listen?

Caring Enough to Understand

Everett Leadingham, Editor

Though this book is designed for group study, it is also intended for personal enjoyment and spiritual growth. A leader's guide is available from your local bookstore or your publisher.

Beacon Hill Press of Kansas City
Kansas City, Missouri

Editor
Everett Leadingham
Associate Editor
Charlie L. Yourdon
Executive Editor
Merritt J. Nielson

Copyright 2003
Beacon Hill Press of Kansas City
Kansas City, Missouri

ISBN: 083-412-0070
Printed in the United States of America

Cover Design:
Michael Walsh

10   9   8   7   6   5   4   3   2   1

Contents

The Christian Witness Amid Pluralism

by Jim L. Bond

THE RELIGIOUS PLURALISM that abounds in our world is not new. Throughout its history, Christianity has existed within a pluralistic milieu. The Early Church emerged within the context of mystery religions, polytheism, gnosticism, and various cults and philosophies, and all were viewed as threats. Speaking to the leaders of the Ephesian church, Paul warned, "Savage wolves will come in among you and will not spare the flock. . . . So be on your guard!" (Acts 20:29, 31).

Such dangers persist today. Christians everywhere are surrounded by people with a wide range of religious beliefs, including Muslims, Hindus, and Buddhists. Some of these are militantly missional, intent on global conquest. Most, however, are good, moral, peaceable members of our communities. How do we as Christians relate to people of other faiths?

□ **With love and respect.** We engage those of other faiths without fear, disrespect, or animosity. We do not attempt to silence them through dogmatism, intimidation, or persuasive logic. Ours is the way of love—patient, kind, and never rude. Our goal in everything is to be like Jesus, even in the way we witness to Muslims. How would He respond to those who perpetrated the tragedy of September 11, 2001? "Love your enemies and pray for those who persecute you," He said (Matthew 5:44). Jesus taught us that love wins. It is His way to build bridges to those of other religions.

☐ **With uncompromising certainty about the uniqueness of Jesus.** Christians today face intense pressure to concede that Jesus is merely one of many ways to God. Our forebears taught us how to answer that charge. They did not denounce those of other faiths, yet they stubbornly refused to syncretize their beliefs about Jesus. "Salvation is found in no one else, for there is no other name under heaven given to men by which we must be saved" (Acts 4:12). We reject any compromise regarding the uniqueness of Jesus.

☐ **With trust in the Spirit who faithfully witnesses to all persons.** We must never forget that all people everywhere are questing to know the true God. Further, the most fundamental of all realities is that through His grace the one and only God is reaching out to every person in our world. "For the grace of God that brings salvation has appeared to all men" (Titus 2:11). We know this as prevenient grace, the grace that precedes salvation. The Triune God takes the initiative, working faithfully in the heart and conscience of every individual to reconcile each one to himself. Everyone, regardless of culture or creed, has the witness of God's grace within—a witness that seeks response.

As we relate to those of other faiths, let's anticipate and embrace every sign of God's grace at work in them. Let's discover places of mutual agreement that can open a crack in the barriers between us. As they begin to respond to the Spirit's overtures, let's be prepared to tell the story of Jesus simply, forthrightly, and lovingly. Then let's trust the Holy Spirit, who alone can convict and convert.

In the warm love of the Spirit, in the knowledge that He is at work, and with trust that He will open doors and guide us, let's give the Good News to people of other religions without fear.

About the Author: Dr. Jim L. Bond is a general superintendent in the Church of the Nazarene. This editorial first appeared in the October, 2002 issue of *Holiness Today*. Used by permission.

CHAPTER 1

Evangelism Is Biblical

by Timothy Pusey

I'LL NEVER FORGET the telephone call I received one day in my office at the church from Bill. He identified himself as a recovering alcoholic. He briefly explained that his son had played baseball at our church's regional college and that, through that experience, he had come to trust our denomination. He knew he needed God and wondered if I would be willing to meet with him.

Of course, I was delighted to meet with him. And Bill accepted Jesus Christ as his personal Savior that day. His conversion marked a radical transformation in his life, and Bill fully embraced that change—hungry for more and more of what the Lord could do in his life. His testimony was so winsome and so powerful that the whole congregation became captivated by God's transforming power as evidenced in Bill's life. His conversion infused new life and new energy into the church.

Isn't it amazing that Bill somehow knew that he could turn to Christ's church for spiritual help, having already concluded that the church would be about the mission of helping lost people find Jesus Christ? He came to that conclusion with minimal background in any church and with no knowledge at all of our local congregation. Yet, even Bill seemed to know that the mission of the church is helping spiritually lost people and that he could trust us to point him in the right direction.

Following Jesus Christ demands that we give our attention to that which captivated the heart of Christ. If we're

going to understand and give adequate reflection to that
which captivated the attention of Christ, we are going to
need to turn to the Scriptures, particularly the Gospels in
the New Testament. Matthew, Mark, Luke, and John tell the
story of the life and ministry of Christ. The remainder of the
New Testament tells us about the ministry of the Early
Church, which was led by the followers of Christ—those
whose lives had been so dramatically transformed and
shaped by the teachings and the person of Jesus. In order to
gain better foundational perspectives for the New Testament, let's begin with the Old Testament.

The Relational, Redemptive God of the Old Testament

Long before God sent His Son to the earth to become the
Savior of humanity, God was making himself known as One
who delighted in relating to His highest creation—human beings. The depth of this most unexpected relationship was evi-
dent even back in the time of Noah. Genesis 6:9 tells us, "Noah
was a righteous man, blameless among the people of his time,
and *he walked with God*" (emphasis added). While God was re-
pulsed with the wickedness of the rest of humanity and was
determined to wipe them from the face of the earth, "Noah
found favor in the eyes of the LORD" (6:8). God made provision
for Noah and his family's lives to be saved. God cared about
those whom He had created. While He would not tolerate bel-
ligerent disobedience, He demonstrated a powerful, protective
love for those who dared to walk with Him.

God spoke to a man named Abram, called him to leave
his homeland and go to a place to which the Lord would direct him (Genesis 12:1-3). God made a covenant with
Abram that would impact all of his descendants. It was a
covenant of blessing—if they would indeed do as God had
instructed them. Thus began the remarkable relationship of
God with the people of Israel, a relationship documented
throughout the pages of the Old Testament. As God contin-

ued to woo the people of Israel into a relationship with Him, He also promised to bless them if they would continue to walk with Him.

In the account of Moses, we discover the redemptive aspect of God's love for His people. The Israelites were living in terrible oppression. They were powerless to free themselves. God had compassion on their plight and, through miraculous means, provided for their freedom and redemption.

This dynamic of God relating to humankind continued throughout the pages of the Old Testament. We read of people, such as Joshua, Gideon, David, and Jonah. God cared about them and wanted them to live in relationship with Him. God was continuing to reach out to the people whom He created and draw them to himself.

The prophets of the Old Testament looked forward to the coming of the Messiah. This Messiah would be a Savior for all the people. Isaiah describes the mission of the Messiah in these words:

The Spirit of the Sovereign LORD is on me,
    because the LORD has anointed me
    to preach good news to the poor.
He has sent me to bind up the brokenhearted,
    to proclaim freedom for the captives
    and release from darkness for the prisoners (61:1).

Luke 4:18-21 records Jesus affirming that He was indeed the One Isaiah was describing in the above passage. The relational, redemptive God revealed in the Old Testament was about to unfold His ultimate plan to reach spiritually lost people.

Lost People Matter to Jesus

As Jesus began His earthly ministry, people soon discovered the tremendous capacity of love that Jesus demonstrated in all His interactions with people. Woven throughout all of what He did was the compelling mission of bringing salvation to spiritually lost people.

□ He gathered a group of 12 disciples from among the

various cross-sections of the population, in order that together they might touch the lives of more lost people.

☐ Jesus performed miracle after miracle, in order to demonstrate God's divine power to change lives.

☐ He talked to people no one else would address, because lost people truly mattered to Him.

☐ Jesus spent time in the homes of sinners, even though He knew that the religious leaders of His day would take Him to task for doing so. Nevertheless, He spent the time because He was about the mission of reaching spiritually lost people.

☐ He was loving and kind to children, who were generally ignored in their culture, because He knew that children needed a Savior too.

☐ Our Lord kept going at times when He needed to escape and be refueled in the presence of the Heavenly Father. He was willing to face the crowds one more time, because He truly cared that there were people in that crowd who would be lost eternally if they did not hear the Good News that He had come to deliver.

☐ Jesus was an advocate for broken people in front of those who were harsh and judgmental.

☐ He told captivating stories to thousands of people, in order that they might somehow grasp that He had come to bring them salvation.

Let's examine three of those wonderful stories (called "parables") that Jesus told in order to communicate His great love for spiritually lost people. Jesus told these stories in response to sharp criticism from the Pharisees and teachers of the Law, who were unhappy that He dared to be seen with ungodly people. To them, it seemed preposterous that someone who represented himself as a godly man would dare contaminate himself by being in the presence, or worse yet, the homes of reputedly sinful people. Jesus didn't see it that way at all. He saw it as His mission to go to those who needed His help the most.

The first of these three stories is the parable of the lost

sheep (Luke 15:3-7). It describes a rancher who owns 100 sheep but is missing 1. Such a rancher would leave the 99 and go searching for the 1. And wonderful delight is shared with others when the missing sheep is found.

In the parable of the lost coin (Luke 15:8-10), a woman loses 1 of 10 silver coins in her possession. She calls an all-out search to find the missing coin. When the coin is found, she calls others to join her in celebrating.

In the familiar parable of the lost son in Luke 15:11-32 (often called the parable of the "prodigal" son), an ambitious, rather self-serving young man asks for his inheritance early, leaves home, and squanders the money in a wild lifestyle. He eventually finds himself destitute and asks if he can return to his home in the status of a hired hand. His father is so overwhelmed with sheer delight that the son had returned he welcomes the son back into the home with all the privileges he ever had as a son. The dad calls all their friends together and has the servants prepare a huge feast to celebrate.

If there was ever any doubt of what Jesus thought about the significance of evangelism, these three stories leave no room for wondering. Jesus' life mission was to reach lost people. Lost people mattered to Him. Above all other things, above all other priorities, above all other agendas, lost people mattered to Jesus.

Christ ultimately proved such love by His willingness to go to the Cross. One of the most beloved scriptures of all time communicates this. "For God so loved the world that he gave his one and only Son, that whoever believes in him shall not perish but have eternal life. For God did not send his Son into the world to condemn the world, but to save the world through him" (John 3:16-17).

The last several chapters of each of the Gospels paint the picture of such tremendous love. Christ endured grueling agony because He loved sinful people so much. Even when He hung on the Cross in excruciating pain, Jesus ministered to the thief hanging on the cross next to His (see Luke

23:32-43). He lived in order that people might be reconciled
to the Heavenly Father, and His death sealed the deal.

I heard recently about a 59-year-old man with a great
love for his 37-year-old son, who had cerebral palsy. As a
teenager, this disabled son had experienced the joy of partic-
ipating with his father in a race. The dad had run and
pushed the cart which held the cherished son whose legs
could never carry him on any kind of race. It so empowered
the son to feel "normal" that the father committed to doing
more of it. Eventually the father, at nearly 60 years of age,
took his son with him through the Ironman Triathlon—one
of the most grueling of all distance races, which combines
bicycling, swimming, and running. The son rode on a special seat on the bike, was pulled by his father in a small raft
through the ocean waters, and was pushed in a cart as the
father ran. The physical strength needed by the father to
carry this out for the son was mind-boggling. Yet, love
pushed him forward. As inspiring as this father's love was
for his son, far greater is the love that Jesus demonstrated for
people like you and me, who were lost and hopeless and
needing a Savior.

The Early Church Catches the Spirit

When the resurrected Jesus was preparing to leave His
disciples, He entrusted to them the continuation of His mission. It was an awesome moment for them. They had witnessed the life of Jesus and heard His phenomenal teachings.
They had seen Him perform miracles. They watched in disbe-
lief as Jesus was arrested, beaten, and crucified. And they
were caught by surprise and unfathomable delight as they
became witnesses of His resurrection. Now Jesus was ready
to commission them to continue His work in this world.

Then Jesus came to them and said, "All authority in
heaven and on earth has been given to me. Therefore go
and make disciples of all nations, baptizing them in the
name of the Father and of the Son and of the Holy Spirit,
and teaching them to obey everything I have command-

ed you. And surely I am with you always, to the very end of the age" (Matthew 28:18-20).

This Great Commission (as the above passage is often called) leaves no mistaking of the purpose and mission for these followers of Jesus Christ. They were to share the good news of salvation through Jesus Christ. They were to love the lost just as Jesus did.

For such a task, Jesus did not leave them without resources. They were promised the gift of the Holy Spirit, and through the Holy Spirit would come power sufficient for the task of sharing with all people the good news of salvation through Jesus. Jesus left them with this challenge:

"Do not leave Jerusalem, but wait for the gift my Father promised, which you have heard me speak about. . . . You will receive power when the Holy Spirit comes on you; and you will be my witnesses in Jerusalem, and in all Judea and Samaria, and to the ends of the earth" (Acts 1:4, 8).

Motivated by a Christ-inspired love for the lost and empowered by the Holy Spirit, the followers of Jesus set out to share the good news of salvation with others. The Book of Acts tells account after account of the exploits of these people, who soon began to be called "Christians" and who together comprised the Early Church.

Peter, under the anointing of the Holy Spirit, spoke boldly to a crowd in Jerusalem, calling them to repent and be baptized in the name of Jesus Christ (Acts 2:38-39). Three thousand became believers in that day alone. This message became the passion of Peter's life and ministry. While the message of salvation was shared first only among the Jews, God revealed to Peter that this promise was for all people (see Acts 10:34-35).

The geographical boundaries of this Good-News-sharing extended further and further, and the Church grew in tremendous strides. The apostle Paul began his widespread journeys to proclaim the good news of salvation through Jesus Christ. God blessed and anointed their work, and the Church thrived, despite persecution.

Evangelism was the heartbeat and mission of the Early Church. They put their lives on the line over and over in order to reach others. Nothing would stop them. No one could deter them. No threat was severe enough to make them stop.

This Is Why We Exist

The Great Commission given to the first followers of Christ is our mission today. We are living in this day and age for the purpose of "making disciples of all nations, baptizing them . . . and teaching them to obey everything [Christ] has commanded [us]." It began when Jesus called His first disciples and promised that He would make those fishermen "fishers of men" (Mark 1:17). The challenge was fully delivered in the powerful words of the Risen Christ before He ascended into heaven (Matthew 28:18-20 and Acts 1:8). It is clear that the followers of Jesus Christ are called to bring others to Jesus. That is our reason for being.

It is a call to us personally and it is a call to us corporately as His church. We do not exist in order to serve ourselves. We exist in order to reach others. The passion which Christ demonstrated in His all-out effort to reach spiritually lost people is the passion we discover as we earnestly seek to follow Him and to be more like Him.

This study is designed to help each participant grasp the importance of reaching lost people and equip him or her with a greater understanding of lost people in our world today. We must understand them if we are going to be most effective in reaching them.

Jesus instructed us to pray for "harvest workers" to give heart and soul to reaching lost people (see Matthew 9:37-38). I want to encourage you today to begin to pray to this end, making yourself available to the Lord to use as He desires. Determine to be part of the "harvest team" and not part of the "labor shortage."

While the challenge seems so much greater than we are, the words of the apostle Paul remind us of the source of our strength in the challenge. "Now to him who is able to do immeasurably more than all we ask or imagine, according to his power that is at work within us, to him be glory in the church and in Christ Jesus throughout all generations, for ever and ever! Amen" (Ephesians 3:20-21).

Scriptures Cited: Genesis 6:8-9; 12:1-3; Isaiah 61:1; Matthew 9:37-38; 28:18-20; Mark 1:17; Luke 4:18-21; 15:3-32; 22:32-43; John 3:16-17; Acts 1:4, 8; 2:38-39; 10:34-35; Ephesians 3:20-21

About the Author: Dr. Timothy Pusey is senior pastor of First Church of the Nazarene, Kansas City, Missouri.

The Changing World Around Us

by C. S. Cowles

AT ABOUT THE TIME I was inaugurated as pastor of a great and historic church in the South, the white middle-class suburb in which it was located began to change in its racial complexion. What started out as a tiny stream of new neighbors soon became a tidal wave as the previous residents moved out virtually *en masse.* And the congregation soon followed.

Today, another voice echoes through that beautiful and spacious sanctuary, built by Christian hands and financed by Christian money. It lifts up not the name of Jesus but Muhammad. In the years since I was pastor, the property has changed hands several times, and is today one of two Black Muslim temples in that city.

The world around us is changing with dizzying speed, and the Church cannot remain unaffected.

The Changing Face of America

I live in San Diego. Unlike nearby Los Angeles, our county is still predominantly Caucasian. Yet, working behind the counter at our neighborhood drugstore are pharmacists and their assistants who come from India, the Near East, China, and Mexico. My mechanic is a Romanian immigrant. My doctor was born, raised, and educated in Afghanistan. My barber fled South Vietnam when the Communists took over. The proprietor of our dry cleaners is an Iranian Christian who fled his country when Ayatollah Khomeini came to power. A realtor-friend emigrated from Lebanon. One colleague with whom I teach is from the Philippines, and another from Ghana. Among our closest neighbors are people of Japanese and African-American descent. Children representing a virtual rainbow of racial backgrounds walk our streets on their way to school.

The foreign-born population of San Diego County surged 41 percent during the 1990s, far outstripping the overall growth in the region. The county is now home to more than 600,000 immigrants, roughly one-fifth of the total population. Half are from Latin America and 33 percent are from Asia. It is not Caucasians but Asians who boast the highest per capita income. Their young excel in school. Although Asian-Americans comprise less than 3 percent of the nation's general population, they make up 12 percent of Harvard's student body, 20 percent of Stanford's, and 30 percent of Berkeley's.

California was the first to become a "minority-majority" state. While Caucasians still comprise the largest ethnic block with 46.7 percent of the population, this percentage is dropping every year. Almost half of California's residents were either born in another country or are children of foreign-born parents. One hundred and thirty languages are spoken by children in the Los Angeles public school system. Though California is the most racially diverse state in the union, Texas, Florida, and New York are not far behind. And these changes can be seen in nearly every city in the country.

There was a time when the majority of Americans could trace their ancestry to the British Isles, but that hasn't been true in more than a century. Latinos, for instance, now comprise the largest minority group in the United States, and that doesn't include the estimated 4 million illegal immigrants or the 4 million American citizens living in Puerto Rico. By 2010 their numbers will grow to 50 million, or one out of six citizens. The Census Bureau estimates that by

2050, one in four will be of Latino descent, with another eight percent of Asian ancestry.

The Changing Face of Religions

Gordon Melton, editor of *The Encyclopedia of American Religions*, lists over 1,500 religious groups in America today, 600 of them non-Christian. Since the United States census does not ask questions about religious affiliation, getting accurate statistics as to the relative strength of the major religious organizations is notoriously difficult. Membership statistics reported by religious groups are sometimes inflated. As the old joke goes, "There are more Baptists in Texas than Texans."

Nevertheless, conservative estimates are that there are just under 2 million Muslims in the United States and Canada, worshiping in 1,000 mosques and Islamic centers. The overwhelming majority are African-Americans, followed by Indo-Pakistanis, and then Arab-Americans. Most American Muslims are Sunnis, but the number of those identifying with the more fundamentalistic and militant Shiite sect is growing. Only 40 percent of the mosques affiliate with the Islamic Society of North America, while the rest remain independent. Ironically, the oldest mosque in the United States is located in the nation's heartland, Cedar Rapids, Iowa. It began as a community center for Muslim immigrants, and became the Mother Mosque of America in 1934.

There are over 2,000 temples and meditation centers serving 2 million Buddhists, mostly Asian immigrants. Forty percent live in California. Four out of five meditation centers are led by Caucasian converts. Americans by the tens of thousands flocked to the Dalai Lama's mass teaching sessions during his tour of the United States in the summer of 1999. His books have topped the best-seller lists. He was welcomed by such celebrities as Oprah Winfrey, Harrison Ford, and Richard Gere. Phil Jackson, Los Angeles Lakers' illustrious coach, whose parents are Pentecostal preachers, is a prominent convert to Buddhism, as is Tina Turner. Like their Christian and Islamic counterparts, Buddhists do not form a monolithic block, and are represented by nearly 50 separate organizations.

There are, in addition, some 800 Hindu and Sikh temples scattered across the country. Hinduism is the other major Eastern religion, found mainly in India.

The Changing Face of the Church

That the influx of immigrants and the proliferation of non-Christian religious groups present the American church with a challenge is an understatement. There are currently more Muslims in the United States than Presbyterians, more Buddhists than Assembly of God members, and more Hindus than Episcopalians. While non-Christian religions have proliferated, mainline Protestant churches have suffered significant declines in membership and attendance. Surprisingly, given its large visibility and influence in American culture, a smaller percentage of Roman Catholics attend mass every Sunday today than at the close of World War II.

Diana Eck has encapsulated this massive shift in the religious profile of the United States in the complete title of her book, *A New Religious America: How a "Christian Country" Has Now Become the World's Most Religiously Diverse Nation.*[1] Her vision of a pluralistic religious landscape has been enthusiastically embraced by many who are eager to affirm a more tolerant and inclusive society.

There is a major flaw, however, in Eck's premise. The United States has never been a religiously diverse country, and is less so now. The decline in mainline church membership has been more than offset by the phenomenal growth of Evangelical and Pentecostal churches over the last three decades. The American Religious Identification Survey of 2001, conducted by the Graduate Center of the City University of New York, found that 52 percent of adults identified themselves as Protestant, 24.5 percent as Catholic, and 14.1 percent as having no religion. Jews and Muslims remain relatively small groups, with Jews representing 1.3 percent of the population, and Muslims less than 1 percent.

The religious groups making the largest gains since 1990 were neither Muslims nor Buddhists but Evangelicals and Pentecostals. Though reliable figures are hard to come by, some studies have found that far more people from non-Christian religions are converting to Christianity than the reverse. This process will only continue as assimilation within the dominant culture increases. Forty-two percent of those who call themselves evangelical, or "born again," say they converted from another religion or had no religion. Even if Jews, Muslims, Buddhists, Hindus, Taoists, and Sikhs continue to grow at their present rate, in 20 years they will still number less than 7 percent of the total population, about the same as in Europe today.

Eck's book also overlooks the fact that a high percentage of the more than 1 million new immigrants who have poured into the United States annually, since the passage of the landmark Immigration Act of 1965, have been Christian. Seventy percent of new immigrants to New York over the last decade have been Christian, as well as over half of all Asians moving to California. They not only form their own churches but infuse existing churches with new life and vitality.

South Korea, for instance, has enjoyed a continuous revival, unmatched anywhere in the world, since the Korean War. Seoul is home to the world's largest church with nearly 750,000 members, led by its founder, Paul Chongi Cho. There are nearly 2,500 Korean immigrant churches in the United States, and two-thirds of these are Presbyterian. I had the privilege of being the guest preacher many times at the Korean Presbyterian Church in Boise, Idaho, where services are held in both Korean and English. It serves a small but prosperous Korean immigrant community.

There are close to 1,000 Chinese Protestant churches in the United States. My father, who was raised in South China by missionary parents and spoke Cantonese fluently, pastored

the Chinese Nazarene Church in Los Angeles for a number of
years, preaching in Chinese and English. It was in his church
that I preached my first sermon. His memorial service was
held in the Chinese church where he worshiped during the
last decade of his life, with his Chinese pastor officiating.

Ministry Amid Racial Diversity

One of the encouraging sociological changes of the last
couple of decades has been the tapering off of the "white
flight" of churches from the inner city where immigrants
and minorities tend to congregate. For one thing, cities are
running out of racially homogenous neighborhoods where
churches can relocate. More importantly, many churches are
reevaluating their mission and their reason for existence.
They are coming to see the influx of racially diverse populations, not as a threat but as a marvelous opportunity for
evangelism and ministry. They do not have to journey overseas to engage in missionary activity but simply go next door.

An increasing number of churches are welcoming their
new neighbors into their fellowship. Many offer worship
services in two or more languages in order to minister to
those who do not speak English. Others are following the
lead of the "mother church" of the Church of the Nazarene,
Los Angeles First, which for decades has had multiple self-
contained ethnic congregations meeting under their roof. In
some multiethnic local churches, the immigrant congregations have outstripped the mother church in attendance,
evangelism, and giving.

One of the most important discoveries we make about
our new neighbors of diverse races and religions is that
many of them hunger for God and salvation. They are often
lonely, feel disoriented, and are disconnected. They long for
a welcoming hand, and for assistance in adjusting to a new
land and culture. They yearn for community, for a sense of
belonging, for the kind of spiritual support that the Church
is uniquely equipped to offer.

As we face the challenge of non-Christian religions in

our community, we ought not to feel the least intimidated by them, much less should we assume that their adherents have no interest in our faith and witness. Two thousand years of missional experience has taught us that the truth of the gospel of Jesus Christ, when presented intelligently, winsomely, and lovingly, holds great appeal to people longing for the assurance of salvation that their religions cannot give. They yearn for freedom from the tyranny of sin, and the hope of eternal life that can be found only in the Good News. There's something about Jesus that impacts human hearts at levels no other religion can touch.

Though devoted to the worship of Allah, Lamin Sanneh became intrigued by the fact that the Koran testifies to Jesus Christ as a prophet of God. Yet, it also claimed that not Jesus but someone else was crucified in His place. Furthermore, the Koran flatly dismisses the New Testament proclamation that Jesus is the divine Son of God. Lamin wondered how the Koran could acknowledge that Jesus was a true prophet, and yet reject as scandalous the claim that He was God in human form. How could a genuine prophet of God be so mistaken? These questions sent him on a quest to find out all he could about Christ. The prospect of what he might discover and how that would change his life, however, filled him with such fear that he asked fellow Muslims to pray he would be delivered from his fascination with Jesus.

Nevertheless, the questions persisted. Suppose Jesus did die on the Cross, and suppose God intended it to be so; how would that change our understanding of God? If Jesus really was the Son of God, and if He really did die on the Cross, that would mean God himself had expressed solidarity with humanity at its deepest levels. In a world shattered by suffering, the Cross spoke to the very center of existence. Christ's suffering was a full-blooded demonstration of the depths of God's love for the human race. And if God rescued Jesus from death by raising Him, as the Gospels report, then that means death has been defeated and there is really life after death.

The breakthrough came when a friend gave Lamin a Bible. He began reading the New Testament voraciously. The Book of Acts convinced him of the veracity of Christian claims regarding Jesus' crucifixion and resurrection. In Romans, he encountered for the first time the fantastic teaching of justification by faith. He was stunned by God's kindness in extending grace to sinners. While reading Romans, he felt liberated, released from his crippling incapacity to please God.

"When we really come to know God's love as expressed in Christ," he says, "we want to testify to it and to place ourselves at the service of God and our fellows." He is currently a tenured professor of Missions and World Christianity at Yale University. His scholarly works on East-West and Muslim-Christian issues have proven to be a valuable resource for those called to transcultural missionary work, especially among Muslims.[2]

Stories like this can be told from every part of the world and out of every religion. Jesus was speaking both prophetically and pragmatically when He said, "I, when I am lifted up . . . , will draw all men to myself" (John 12:32). There's something infinitely compelling about Jesus. And in our changing world, that is very good news.

Notes:

1. Diana L. Eck, *A New Religious America: How a "Christian Country" Has Now Become the World's Most Religiously Diverse Nation* (San Francisco: Harper San Francisco, 2001).

2. Kelly Monroe, ed., *Finding God at Harvard* (Grand Rapids: Zondervan, 1996), 191-97.

Scriptures Cited: John 12:32

About the Author: Dr. C. S. Cowles teaches religion and philosophy at Point Loma Nazarene University, San Diego, California.

CHAPTER 3

Grace Is Always Working
by David L. McKenna

GRACE, THE FREE and undeserved gift of God by which we are saved, is at the heart and soul of Wesleyan belief and experience. This is not as obvious as it may seem. Christian theology balances on a pinpoint between viewing truth from a perspective of grace or strictness. To maintain that balance is not easy. In some generations, the more gentle doctrine of grace prevails. In others, the relentless pursuit of truth seems more harsh.

Puritan preaching in Colonial America back in the 1700s, for instance, is remembered for its stern truth. Jonathan Edwards, a great preacher of that era, is best known for his sermon "Sinners in the Hands of an Angry God." Edwards also preached the grace of God, but in the hard-nosed Calvinist mind of the Puritans, it tended to lose its beauty as a free and universal gift.

On the other extreme, we are firsthand witnesses of cheap grace in our day. In place of Jonathan Edwards's hell fire and brimstone preaching of hard truth, we have the soft soap and sugary preaching of easy grace.

Wesleyans do not have a corner on grace. We do, however, have a responsibility to maintain the Spirit-guided balance between grace and stern truth. Our task is complicated by the fact that biblical grace is a paradox. At one and the same time, it is a gift that is costly and yet free. Its cost is written in the cross of Jesus Christ, and its free provision is written in God's "whosoever will" (Revelation 22:17, KJV). Wesleyans also believe that grace is full as well as free. "Full," in this context, refers to the grace that is at work in every person, even before salvation, as the Holy Spirit uses an infinite variety of means to lead us to God. Furthermore, it is the fullness of grace that makes our sanctification possible.

Jesus himself is our model. He is described as a person "full of grace and truth" (John 1:14). This is the defining characteristic of spiritual beauty in human personality. To stress either grace or truth is to lose the "fullness" that gives our witness its distinguishing quality. Here again, our Wesleyan emphasis upon the work of the Holy Spirit comes into view. Only with His discerning mind can we keep the balance.

John Wesley himself shows us the fullness of grace in his own spiritual journey. In his early life history, we see the gift of grace shaping him for one of the most effective and far-reaching ministries in human history—leading him to God, saving him in Christ, and sanctifying him through the Holy Spirit. Wesley would be the first to reject the notion that we should be carbon copies of him, but with his confidence in God's grace, he would not hesitate to recommend that we accept the gift, full and free.

Leading Grace

In the life history of John Wesley leading up to Aldersgate, we see the dimensions of prevenient or "leading" grace at work. Prevenient grace is defined as the grace that "goes before us." It is *preventing grace* that kept John Wesley from gross sin; *awakening grace* that stirred in him the thirst for inward holiness; *surprising grace* by which God revealed himself through unexpected events. C. S. Lewis recounted how God kept surprising him when he was resisting the faith. "God is very unscrupulous," he wrote. "He makes sure that open Bibles are lying on tables wherever I go." Prevenient grace is also convicting grace, which made Wesley weep because of unbelief. It is the leading grace that brought him to faith in Christ and Christ alone.

Prevenient grace is the Wesleyan answer to the Calvinist doctrine of predestination. Without diluting the nature of human sin or the sovereignty of God's will, we believe with Wesley that grace is "free in all, and free for all." Or as another Christian has said, "It is like the air we breathe or the wind that blows in our faces." God's prevenient grace goes before us—awakening in us a thirst for God, surprising us with His providence, convicting us of unbelief, and leading us to trust in Christ and Christ alone.

We need to rediscover the meaning of prevenient grace in our own lives as well as in the lives of people we are called to serve. The heavy weight of Freudian psychology has given us a negative fixation on our past. Prevenient grace gives us a different picture of our past.

Recent writers have recommended that we return to the practice of 18th-century Methodists and keep a journal of our spiritual walk. To begin, the suggestion is that we go back to the earliest memories of our lives and note the "marker events" that help us define who we are and how we got where we are today. Chapters in our journal are proposed for ages 1 to 6, from 6 to 12, 12 to 20, 20 to 40, 40 to 55, 55 to 70, and 70 until we are no longer able. The authors suggest that we name each chapter and then ask the question, "How was the Spirit of God at work in my life during this time?" Such a promising question is a radical departure from a downcast, self-excusing attitude toward our life history.

Prevenient grace takes the mystery out of what God is doing in our lives. It also changes our view of people, institutions, movements, and cultures in the world. God is no arbitrary ruler, capricious gambler, or absentee landlord as far as our eternal destiny is concerned. In every person and in every movement, He is leading, convicting, pursuing, and drawing us toward His saving grace. God uses every means at His disposal to get our attention and lead us to faith. So, our spiritual journey may seem tortuous and long, but make no mistake—God's will for us is good, and His goal for us is our salvation.

Saving Grace

At the age of 35, John Wesley went "very unwillingly" to a place on narrow Aldersgate Street in the north of London where someone was reading from Luther's *Preface to the Epistle to the Romans.* Into the readiness of Wesley's heart, saving grace broke through to prompt this testimony, "I felt my heart strangely warmed; I felt I did trust in Christ, Christ alone, for salvation, and an assurance was given me that He had taken away my sins, even mine, and saved me from the law of sin and death."

Wesley's Aldersgate experience is more than a "gust of feeling." In it, we see the gift of God's saving grace with which any believer identifies. Wesley's own testimony reminds us that saving grace, through the work of the Holy Spirit, *regenerates* us in the image of Christ, *justifies* us in the Cross of Christ, and *assures* us of our salvation in the love of Christ.

Saving grace regenerates us in the image of Christ. Regeneration is the work of God through His Holy Spirit by which we are made new creatures in the image of Christ. Without doubt, Aldersgate was an emotional experience. For the first time, he could admit feeling as well as fact, heart as well as head, surprise as well as order, and warmth as well as cold. Our spiritual experience is never complete without the "burst of feeling," the "surprise of miracle," and the "warmth of love."

Regenerating grace makes us whole persons as well as new creatures in the image of Christ. As John Wesley illustrates so well, the strange, heartwarming experience balances the disciplined mind and obedient will that he brought to Aldersgate. Wesley needed the warmth of love to be a whole person. Our need today is just the opposite. We need the disciplined mind and obedient will to balance out emotional experiences and spiritual subjectivity.

Saving grace justifies us in the cross of Christ. We stand before a monumental truth that is being neglected today. Justification by faith takes us directly to the saving grace of Jesus

Christ. John Stott, in his book *The Cross of Christ*, presents these helpful images for understanding the full meaning of our salvation:

- □ *Propitiation* is the image of the shrine. Here is Christ's atoning sacrifice to appease the wrath of God that we deserve.
- □ *Redemption* is the image of the marketplace. Here Christ buys us back and sets us free from the captivity of sin.
- □ *Justification* is the image of the law court. Here Christ becomes our substitute and accepts the sentence of our guilt.
- □ *Reconciliation* is the image of the home. Here Christ restores broken relationships for those who are alienated from the Father.

For Wesley, Aldersgate meant a shift in the center of gravity for his soul. No longer would he rely upon the works of intellectualism, moralism, ritualism, or mysticism for his salvation. Neither a disciplined mind nor an obedient will can justify us before God. As Paul wrote to the Galatians, "I do not set aside the grace of God, for if righteousness could be gained through the law, Christ died for nothing!" (2:21).

There is nothing to pay, and we cannot make a contribution. Yet, as John Stott says, "We resent the idea that we cannot earn—or at least contribute to our own salvation. So, we stumble, as Paul put it, over the stumbling block of the cross of Christ" (see Romans 9:30-33).

Our need is the perspective on justifying grace that Toplady gives us in the hymn "Rock of Ages":

Nothing in my hands I bring,
Simply to Thy cross I cling;
Naked, come to Thee for dress,
Helpless, look to Thee for grace;
Foul, I to the fountain fly,
Wash me, Savior, or I die!

Each of us asks the question, "How can I be sure of my salvation?" *Saving grace assures us of our salvation in the love of Christ.* When nothing in classical theology could define his Aldersgate experience, Wesley turned to the Scriptures for help. He discovered the meaning of Aldersgate in Romans 8:16, "The Spirit himself testifies with our spirit that we are God's children." Before Aldersgate, he could not answer "Yes" when asked if he had the witness of the Spirit that he was a child of God. After Aldersgate, he answered "Yes" with complete confidence.

If Wesleyan theology has a litmus test for faith, it is the "witness of the Spirit." In this truth is the Wesleyan doctrine of assurance that joins prevenient grace as unique contributions to biblical theology and our Christian faith.

Certainty of salvation is always a dilemma. Although I was brought up in a church whose theology was obliquely Wesleyan, I never heard the doctrine of assurance emphasized as a distinctive of our heritage. Perhaps this is why I struggled for years with the dread of displeasing God, losing my faith, and going to hell.

At first, I thought that Calvinists had a corner on certainty. Then, I learned that John Calvin himself wrote that the saint's greatest struggle was the lack of certainty about salvation. Even with irresistible grace and the perseverance of the saints, there was no certainty of salvation until death. Roman Catholics depend upon the church for their certainty; Lutherans depend upon faith; Reformers depend upon doctrine. For the people called Wesleyans, however, our certainty is found in an affirmative answer to the question, "Have you the witness of the Spirit that you are a child of God?" With our affirmation comes His assurance.

Sanctifying Grace

On the way to Aldersgate with John Wesley, we marveled at the evidence of prevenient grace—the grace that prevents us from sin, convicts us of sin, and leads us toward God and Christ. At Aldersgate with Wesley, we stood amazed in the strange and warming presence of saving grace—the grace that regenerates us as new creatures, justifies us before God, and assures us of salvation through the witness of the Spirit. Now, we come to the third towering truth in the Wesleyan trilogy of grace—the experience of sanctifying grace.

God's grace is the common denominator in each of these experiences. In Wesley's day, the announcement that God's grace was "free in all, and free to all" had the sound of spiritual reveille. Calvinism restricted the grace of God, deism had depersonalized it, Lutheranism had objectified it, Moravianism had mystified it, and Anglicanism had forgotten it. The Wesleys, however, made the free gift of God's grace the keynote of sermon and song.

Equally important to our understanding of grace is the work of the Holy Spirit; we cannot forget that it is the person of the Holy Spirit through whom grace flows.

When we speak of sanctifying grace, we begin with the evidence of *growing grace.* No one contests the fact that the Holy Spirit is given to the believer at the time of justification. For Wesleyans, it is also the time when the dynamic process of entire sanctification begins.

Growing grace is always painful. In the Gospel of John we read, "And of his fulness have all we received, and grace for grace" (1:16, KJV). None of us is exempt from the fault lines that also appeared in Wesley after Aldersgate—moments of depression, moments of doubt, conflicts with people, and failures in witness. Yet, we must remember that faith gets lazy if all is well and good all of the time. As painful as it seems, our faith only grows when we confront a contradiction that requires us to expand our circle of trust. At best, we hobble toward holiness; but if we keep our insatiable thirst for God along the way, He will give us grace to handle our contradictions. So often, during times of struggle, I find myself humming the song:

> *He giveth more grace when the burdens grow greater;*
> *He sendeth more strength when the labors increase.*
> *To added affliction He addeth His mercy;*
> *To multiplied trials, His multiplied peace.*

His love has no limit; His grace has no measure.
His pow'r has no boundary known unto men.
For out of His infinite riches in Jesus,
He giveth, and giveth, and giveth again!

(Annie Johnson Flint)

Wesley's analogy of a house to characterize the full scope of the Christian experience is most enlightening. Repentance, he said, is the porch, justification is the doorway, and sanctification is the hallowing of all of the rooms of the house. I would only add that prevenient grace is the pathway leading to the porch.

May God forgive us for making the experience of sanctifying grace a point of theological controversy, a signal of spiritual superiority, or a stopping place along the road of our spiritual journey. Wesley would be the first to call us to grow toward the goal of the experience called "holiness" and never stop growing.

Holiness is so practical and personal when we think of the experience this way: When the incarnate Spirit dwells in us, the motive of Christ's "perfect love" is possible. When the Spirit speaks through us, the Word of Christ is heard. When the Spirit moves through us, the grace of Christ is known. When the Spirit acts through us, the glory of God is revealed.

Giving Grace

Resting in the power and presence of His sanctifying grace does not mean that we stop on our journey of faith. Immediately after Wesley experienced the heart strangely warmed, he began praying for those who had despised him and persecuted him. Wesley defined the "witness of the Spirit" as a two-sided coin. On one side is the witness of the Spirit that we are the children of God—the inward evidence of piety. On the other side is the witness of the Spirit that we are obedient to His will—the outward evidence of mercy.

Giving grace is the final evidence of the Spirit-filled life. Jesus taught us the meaning of giving grace in the parable of the man who was forgiven of a major debt by the king but refused to forgive a brother who owed him a pittance (see Matthew 18:23-35). Consequently, the grace that he received was canceled by the king. To be fully operative, grace freely received must be grace freely given. Likewise, we cannot claim the fullness of the Spirit without showing the fruits of giving grace.

Conclusion

Aldersgate Street is a place. The site on Aldersgate Street where John Wesley had his heart strangely warmed, however, is unknown. The best that Methodist historians can do is put up a plaque at the entrance to the street for visitors to see. If the exact site were known, we might be tempted to make it a shrine, worship the symbol, and lose the meaning of the event. Aldersgate is a marker event that cannot be duplicated in kind. Rather, it symbolizes a spiritual journey with marker events and continuing experiences.

Wesleyans are people together on that journey. On the road to Aldersgate, we are amazed at the evidence of God's leading grace; at a place called Aldersgate, we feel our hearts strangely warmed by the power of saving grace; and on the road after Aldersgate, we are filled with the Holy Spirit through His sanctifying grace. All along the way, there is the assurance of our salvation. As a continuing question, Wesleyans ask themselves and each other, "Have you the witness of the Spirit that you are a child of God?" Wherever we are on the journey, amazing grace lets us answer, "Yes."

Scriptures Cited: Matthew 18:23-35; John 1:14; Romans 8:16; 9:30-33; Galatians 2:21; Revelation 22:17

About the Author: This chapter has been excerpted from *What a Time to Be Wesleyan!* (Kansas City: Beacon Hill Press of Kansas City, 1999) by David McKenna. Used by permission, all rights reserved. Dr. McKenna, a noted scholar and public speaker, is a former president of Asbury Theological Seminary in Wilmore, Kentucky.

CHAPTER 4

The Work of the Holy Spirit

by David L. McKenna

THEOLOGICAL CONFUSION, political contradiction, and personal chaos are threats to the integrity of our Christian witness in the 21st century. A tendency toward a "generic evangelical theology" in which biblical distinctives are lost in the desire to be acceptable to the contemporary mind is evidence of our theological confusion. The temptation to be aligned with partisan movements that have selective moral agendas or ignore the whole counsel of God exposes our political contradictions. And evidence that evangelical Christians suffer the same problems, ranging from abuse to addiction, as the general population tells us that we are also victims of personal chaos.

Without apology, I believe that scriptural holiness defined in biblical and Wesleyan terms is a Spirit-guided corrective for our theological confusion, political contradiction, and personal chaos. This does not mean that Wesleyans are exempt from these problems or hold an exclusive answer to their solution. I do believe, however, that we bring to these issues a biblically based understanding of the teaching ministry of the Holy Spirit that is practical for today and creative for tomorrow.

A map is better than a rulebook for guiding Christians through the "no-man's land" of a hostile culture. We have that map in the Word of God. According to the promise of Christ, it is the unique teaching ministry of the Holy Spirit who leads us in the task of tracing the map of revelation on the new frontiers of Christian fidelity and witness. Then, when the map of revelation is unfolded to guide our faith and life, it is the gyroscopic balance of the Holy Spirit that keeps us on center and heading in the right direction.

Wesleyan theology brings three emphases to the map work. *First, we see the work of the Holy Spirit as a dynamic experience* in which He not only cleanses us as an act of grace but enlightens us as a continuing process. *Second, we see the Scriptures as "God-breathed" in their inspiration,* meaning that the Living Word is interactive with the continuing revelation of truth through the mind of the Holy Spirit. *Third, we see ourselves as learners under the teaching of the Holy Spirit* as we submit our minds as well as our hearts to Him.

For these reasons, Wesleyans pay particular attention to the often-neglected promise of Jesus that "the Holy Spirit, whom the Father will send in my name, will teach you all things" (John 14:26). "He will convict the world of guilt in regard to sin and righteousness and judgment" (16:8). "He will tell you what is yet to come" (16:13).

Teaching Us Everything

Behind Jesus' promise that the Holy Spirit will teach us all things are three working principles that shape our Christian worldview.

First, our Christian worldview is centered in Jesus Christ. No question is more important than to ask a person, "What is the truth that holds your world together?" For a Christian, the unequivocal answer is "Jesus Christ." When He promises that the Holy Spirit "will guide [us] into all truth" (John 16:13), Jesus puts himself at the center of that truth. A Christian is a person who believes that all human history turns on the event of the Incarnation when Jesus Christ, the Son of God, became flesh in order to redeem us. No one else can be at the center. This fact is reinforced by Jesus' word that even the Holy Spirit will not speak of himself, but only of what He has heard Christ speak. He shows us only what

Christ has shown Him and He leads us only into the truth that Christ has revealed to Him. It was this fact that led the apostle Paul to write to the Colossians, "In him all things hold together" (1:17).

For those of us who believe in Jesus Christ, this truth may seem obvious. Facts give us pause. At one time, there was common agreement among scholars that "all truth is God's truth." But in the 18th century, we entered into what is known as the Age of Enlightenment. Both theologians and philosophers moved God out of the center of the universe and Christ out of the center of truth. Presumably, the "enlightened" human mind took their place. Miraculous advances along with tragic consequences followed. Scientific advancements credited to the freedom of the human mind have dazzled us, but the moral consequences have confounded us. Even now, predictions of the future are turning upon scientific discoveries in chips, genes, and atoms. Unless God in Jesus Christ is the center of all truth, human knowledge will never hold together.

Second, our Christian worldview is comprehensive. When we make our commitment to the centrality of Jesus Christ, we commit ourselves to much more. We commit ourselves to the Bible as the revelation of the nature of God, the interpretation of human history, and the prediction of human destiny.

When I was a college freshman, my theology professor described the work of the Holy Spirit in our lives by taking a thread from his blue suit. He said, "If you take any thread from this suit and put it under a microscope, you will see that it has the tone and texture of the whole cloth." Applying his illustration, he went on to say, "That is how the Holy Spirit works in our lives. Every fiber of our being is true to the tone and texture of the Spirit-filled life."

The same can be said for our Christian worldview. When Jesus promises that the Spirit will "guide [us] into all truth," He means that there are no facts, ideas, notions, values, opinions, discoveries, or events that are not made captive to "the mind of Christ" (1 Corinthians 2:16*b*) by the Spirit of truth.

Third, our Christian worldview is creative. Even though our view of the world is centered in Jesus Christ and comprehensive of all truth, it does not mean that we have all of the answers or are exempt from surprise. To the contrary, our Christian worldview is continuously being re-created as the Holy Spirit teaches us how to process new information through spiritual discernment. One theologian proposed that new information coming into our field may be processed in one of three ways. If the information is compatible with the Word of God, we integrate it into our Christian worldview. If it conflicts with the Word of God, we refute it with reasoned understanding after serious study. But if the new information is a mystery that is neither compatible nor conflicting with the Word of God, we hold it for further investigation. In each case, the Holy Spirit is our Teacher, helping us discern how new information is related to our faith position.

Convicting the World of Sin

Information is not morally neutral. The more information we have, the more complex are the moral decisions that we must make. While we may prefer the simplicity of either/or choices in a black-and-white world, the age of information in the 21st century will not give us this luxury. Rather than simply sorting our choices into either/or categories, we will have to work along an ethical continuum that requires that we consider multiple options, anticipate contagious implications, and weigh far-reaching consequences. The burden will be too much for us unless we have the discerning mind of the Spirit of truth. Jesus anticipates our need in His promise, "When [the Counselor] comes, he will convict the world of guilt in regard to sin and righteousness and judgment" (John 16:8).

In this promise, Jesus gives us the essential elements of an ethical system for making moral decisions as Christians.

An ethical system requires three parts: a standard for judging right and wrong; a sanction that affirms right and condemns wrong; and a consequence that rewards right and punishes wrong.

The change in public attitude toward premarital sex illustrates how an ethical system works—and how it breaks down. Not many years ago there was the standard, supported by a moral consensus, that premarital sex was wrong. Public opinion confirmed the standard by a sanction that affirmed young people who deferred sex until marriage and reproved those who failed to live up to the standard. Consequences reinforced both the standard and the sanction. Young people who participated in premarital sex lived with the fear of pregnancy, and those who became pregnant served as examples of the consequences of the broken standard. Then, in the 1960s, the standard was challenged by the changing ideas of the times, the sanctions were lost in the moral revolution glamorized by the media, and the consequences were lifted by the pill. Today, in the public mind, premarital sex is accepted as an individual preference without social condemnation and little fear of pregnancy. An ethical system has broken down.

A vital function of the Holy Spirit is to teach us the ethics as revealed by Jesus Christ that undergird our Christian worldview.

First, our moral standard is belief in Jesus Christ. According to Scripture, sin separates us from God. Behind this standard is the fact that our human nature rebels against God by rejection of Jesus Christ. The Holy Spirit's task is to convict the world of its sin and remind us that there is no other standard by which human behavior is judged.

Second, our moral sanction is righteousness through Jesus Christ. If I were asked to name the 10 books that have had the most influence upon my life, I would put close to the top of the list Charles Sheldon's novel *In His Steps.* As a teenager seeking to know the will of God, I shall never forget the question the characters in the book chose as the guide for all of their life decisions: "What would Jesus do?" Time and time again, I have asked that question when confronted with moral choices, large and small. Without fail, the question has taken me deeply into the mind and spirit of Jesus Christ. More often than not, the Holy Spirit brings from my memory an event or teaching from the life of Jesus that becomes a safe and sure guide for my decision. The Holy Spirit will always convict us if we embrace any standard that is not compatible with the mind and Spirit of Jesus Christ.

Third, our moral consequence is judgment by Jesus Christ. We must be constantly reminded that all humankind is accountable to God. The cross of Jesus Christ is the symbol of His judgment upon sin and Satan. In the Cross, there is full freedom from the condemnation of sin, but there is also the continuing judgment upon the works and ways of every individual and institution on earth.

As our Teacher, the Holy Spirit saves us from arrogance by reminding us that all of our works stand under the judgment of God. Christians who believe that they are doing the work and will of God especially need this humility. Our best efforts are usually flawed by mixed motives and limited understanding. We are only commissioned to preach the gospel to the lost; it is the Holy Spirit who is responsible for the results. Humility is the companion of honesty as we submit ourselves to the checks and balances of the Holy Spirit.

Showing Us What Is Coming

Our Christian worldview must include an exciting vision of the future in which we see ourselves playing a significant part. Although all Christians look forward to the time when Christ's purpose will be fulfilled on earth, we quickly divide and fight over the details. Only the Holy Spirit can help us work our way through the minefield and draw a map for others to follow.

We can think of the Holy Spirit acting as a gyroscope. The more powerful the contending forces and the faster it turns, the better balanced the gyroscope becomes. So, as we apply the analogy to the Holy Spirit as our Teacher, we see how He balances contending forces and gives us hope for the future.

First, the Holy Spirit balances our short-term and long-term view of the future. There is no question about the fact that Christianity is a long-term view. By definition, a secular society is limited to the short-term view of this present age. As humans, we lose our ability to foresee the future and make the adjustments needed for changing times. Here is where the Holy Spirit becomes our mentor. He will keep us on alert against the seductive, short-term satisfactions of a secular society. Better yet, He will not let us lose sight of the long-term view that God wants us to see.

The other extreme is to become so fixated on the future that our spirituality becomes mystical and impractical. Rather than becoming immersed in the secular society, we become isolated from it. Here again, the Holy Spirit serves as our mentor in the balancing out of the short- and long-term view. In that delicate balance, we are neither immersed in the secular society nor isolated from its issues. As our Teacher, the Holy Spirit shows us how to live productively, playfully, and purposefully.

Second, the Holy Spirit balances our pessimism and our optimism for the future. Again, the primary truth is that Christianity is guided by the optimism of the Good News. Consistent with God's redemptive plan, our long-term vision sees the transformation of the earth and the consummation of time in the new creation, the new order, and the new kingdom (Isaiah 65:17-25).

Through the mind of the Spirit, we see things to come in the balance between the reality of human sin and the promise of God's grace. In that balance, we are called to be realistic optimists.

Third, the Holy Spirit shows us the balance between process and event in our view of the future. No one doubts that Christianity is known by its events. As we look back to the Incarnation as the turning point in human history, we look forward to the second coming of Christ as the culminating event in human redemption.

For Christians, the greater danger is to focus on the event at the expense of the process. When I was a senior in high school, a traveling evangelist came to our holiness tabernacle. This self-proclaimed doctor brought a large, multicolored chart and a long pointer to the platform with him. On the chart was the cutaway drawing of the Great Pyramid in Egypt. With a dramatic flourish of the pointer, the professor identified the entryway as the symbol of creation and the downward shaft as proof of the Fall. Through the narrow passageways and into the chambers he went with his pointer, tracing by length and space the stages of human history. Finally, he came to a very narrow passageway that he described as the "Age of Reason or the Age of Enlightenment." Then bursting into the secret chamber where the treasures of Tut were found, he shouted, "This is the Second Coming!" You can imagine the impression that he made upon his congregation as he took out his ruler, measured the length of the final passageway, counted the time of the centuries, and then announced with the precision of a scientist, "Jesus Christ is coming again on April 21, 1947!"

Of course, the professor's declaration led to an altar call. Because the meeting took place sometime in March 1947, he had urgency on his side. I went forward to the altar, not praying for salvation, but asking God to delay His coming until I could graduate from high school in June!

The story of the professor illustrates the fact that we can become so fixated on the *event* of redemption that we forget our responsibility for the *process* of redemption. Thus, the writer to the Hebrews said, "Let us hold unswervingly to the hope we profess, for he who promised is faithful. And let us consider how we may spur one another on toward love and good deeds . . . and all the more as [we] see the Day approaching" (10:23-25).

In Love with the Truth

We have come full cycle on the meaning of Jesus' promise for the coming of the Spirit of truth to be our Teacher. The word "truth" is derived from the word "troth"—not unlike the pledge of two lovers who give themselves to each other. If then we want to know the truth, we must be betrothed to the Spirit of truth.

Perhaps as never before, we are being bombarded by so much information from the media that we have trouble sorting out truth from fiction and falsehood. *How do we discern the truth? How do we decide for the truth? How do we stand for the truth?*

No answer will suffice for these questions except as we become students under the teaching of the Holy Spirit. We must experience His cleansing fire, receive His enabling power, and learn His discerning ways. True to our engagement to the Spirit of truth, our task is to bring biblical balance back into the experience of the Spirit-filled life. Without neglecting our feelings or our discipline, we must meet the challenge of the information age with the mind of the Spirit. We have the twofold task of winning souls and winning minds.

If we are true to our biblical trust and our Wesleyan heritage, we will be known in the 21st century as reasonable and disciplined enthusiasts under the teaching of the Holy Spirit.

Scriptures Cited: Isaiah 65:17-25; John 14:26; 16:8, 13; 1 Corinthians 2:16b; Colossians 1:17; Hebrews 10:23-25

About the Author: This chapter has been excerpted from *What a Time to Be Wesleyan!* (Kansas City: Beacon Hill Press of Kansas City, 1999) by David McKenna. Used by permission, all rights reserved. Dr. McKenna, a noted scholar and public speaker, is a former president of Asbury Theological Seminary in Wilmore, Kentucky.

CHAPTER 5

Why Wesleyans Share Their Faith

by David L. McKenna

WESLEYANS ARE A worldly people. Not in the traditional sense of the word but in the scope of their vision for the lost. When John Wesley dared to cross parish boundaries in order to preach in fields and marketplaces, the Anglican hierarchy tried to stop him. In bold response, Wesley invoked the authority of the Great Commission and announced, "I look upon all the world as my parish."[1]

Our world has been turned upside down since Wesley's day. We are fast becoming citizens of a "global village" connected by instant communication. At the same time, we are becoming more diverse in racial, ethnic, social, and religious origins. Our world parish in the 21st century will not be a melting pot of people blending into white, Western, Christian, and Anglo-Saxon sameness, but a salad bowl in which racial, ethnic, gender, social, and religious differences remain intact except for the dressing of our common humanity, which makes them palatable.

Wesleyans who are true to Christ's commission and Wesley's world vision will not shy away from our parish of tomorrow. Out of our history, we bring resources to the changing scene that are enhanced by time and change. *First, we inherit Wesley's willingness to become "vile" in order to preach the gospel of deliverance, recovery, and liberty to the poor.*[2] As he took to the fields and the marketplace, we must

45

venture to those places in our world where human need and spiritual opportunity converge.

Second, we are heirs of Wesley's ability to create a network of ministry for reaching all people. As Wesley rode a circuit around England on horseback, we must ride a circuit around the world by media. We must reclaim the concept of the circuit in the electronic age in order to embrace our world.

Third, as Wesleyans we have received the pattern of our fore-bear's organizational genius for nurturing our converts into spiritual maturity. Its effectiveness for developing discipleship and leadership has never been questioned, and its model keeps reappearing in growing churches and movements. We must rediscover that pattern, and especially the motive that prompted it and the discipline that perpetuated it.

Fourth, from our heritage, we have the legacy of Wesley's conscience for social justice. In the 21st century, issues of social justice on a global scale will continue to be as prickly as a bramble bush. Yet, under the guidance of the Holy Spirit, John Wesley walked with wisdom through thickets no less thorny. By his example, he has much to teach us.

Fifth, and perhaps most of all, we bring his passion to win the lost and his compassion to serve the poor. Wesleyans will cross all boundaries with the message of grace and the motive of love, once again demonstrating the meaning of "faith expressing itself through love" (Galatians 5:6).

With these resources for ministry in the 21st century, how do we, as Wesleyans, become the people who are ready to preach the gospel and serve the poor in all places, at any time?

Compelled by Conviction

Anyone with the slightest sense of adventure will be inspired by the vision of a world parish. To make the vision reality, however, is a different matter. Two natural tendencies take over. One is to settle down in the comfort level of our success at the local level. The other tendency is to rework old territory rather than stretching out to new and uncharted areas.

Our biblical precedent for a world parish counters both of these natural tendencies. In the example of Jesus Christ and the apostle Paul, we see the only motivation that makes sure that our vision of a world parish becomes a reality. By example, they show us what it means to be compelled by conviction.

Jesus opened His public ministry in Capernaum with a busy day of preaching with authority, casting out unclean spirits, healing the sick, and shutting the mouths of demons. Like wildfire, His fame spread throughout Galilee and its surrounding regions. While anticipating rest and renewal through prayer, Jesus was interrupted by Simon and the other disciples who announced, "Everyone is looking for you!" (Mark 1:37).

Weighing the implications of such popularity, Jesus responded with resolution, "Let us go somewhere else—to the nearby villages—so I can preach there also. That is why I have come" (1:38).

Rejecting the temptation to settle down in the comfort of local popularity, Jesus gives us the incentive to "go somewhere else," not only from town to town but also from nation to nation and from continent to continent until the whole world is embraced.

The apostle Paul, in his letter to the Romans, completed the vision of Jesus when he wrote, "It has always been my ambition to preach the gospel where Christ was not known" (Romans 15:20). He might have been content to build upon his popularity among the seven churches of Asia Minor and to rework these territories with the assurance of acceptance and success. Certainly, Paul yearned to minister to the beleaguered Christians in Rome, the very center of pagan opposition. Yet, the vision of God's redemptive plan for a lost world as seen through the eyes of the prophet Isaiah spurred him on. Without the advantage of market research, but with the mind of the Holy Spirit, Paul went "somewhere else." There is no other path to the whole world. We must move on from our places of security and move forward into new and uncharted fields with the name of Christ.

Centuries after Jesus and Paul, John Wesley also had to make a decision. In his journal, he wrote, "God in scripture commands me, according to my power, to instruct the ignorant, reform the wicked, confirm the virtuous. Man forbids me to do this in another's parish. That is, in effect, to do it at all, seeing that I have no parish of my own, nor probably, never shall. Whom then shall I hear, God or man?"[3]

Responding to his own question, Wesley declared, "I look upon all the world as my parish; thus far I mean, that, in whatever part of it I am, I judge it meet, right and my bounden duty to declare unto all that are willing to hear, the glad tidings of salvation."[4]

Move forward two more centuries into the early 1970s. I invited Billy Graham to be our commencement speaker at Seattle Pacific University. Courteously, but without pretenses or apology, Billy explained that each year he received more than 15,000 invitations to speak across the world. A majority of the invitations come from Christian organizations. Dr. Graham said, "I could spend all of my time speaking to groups who would applaud every word, but God has given me opportunities to preach where the name of Christ has not been heard. I would love to be with you, but I can't come."

The next week on radio, I heard Dr. Graham addressing the National Press Club, answering their pointed questions without compromising the gospel. Afterward, I wrote him a note saying, "Now I understand why you turned me down. I want to learn the same lesson."

Commissioned by Grace

It takes an air of audacity to claim that we have a special calling to the whole world. It takes an edge of arrogance to assume that we have something special to say to that world. And it takes a dose of ambition to continue stretching out into uncharted territory where the very name of Christ has not been heard or understood.

Grace makes all of the difference in our claims to witness in a world parish. In ourselves, we find no superior goodness or superior knowledge. We acknowledge that our own righteousness is as filthy rags and our own knowledge is like a clanging cymbal. With Paul, our only claim to offer Christ to others is the gift of grace that God has given us. As he had the commission of grace to preach to the Gentiles, we are commissioned by grace to make the world our parish.

A liberal critic of D. L. Moody once confessed, "He has a right to preach the gospel because he never speaks of a lost soul without a tear in his eye." Paul also had a tear in his eye. He described himself as "minister of Christ Jesus to the Gentiles with the priestly duty of proclaiming the gospel of God" (Romans 15:16). Where grace is involved, whether clergy or laity, we are commissioned to be priests—intercessors who weep and pray for those to whom the gospel is given.

Grace puts its own check on any arrogance about the results of our witness. Each of us would like to display people as trophies of our witness in the world. Paul was not so presumptuous. He sees his priestly responsibility to be offering up the Gentiles before God as an "acceptable sacrifice" (Philippians 4:18). His effectiveness was then sealed by the work of the Holy Spirit as people were redeemed and their witness of grace became the sweet smelling savor of the sacrifice consumed.

John Wesley also saw his world parish through the eyes of grace. Along with Paul, Wesley saw a world parish in which he was a priest interceding for the lost with a tear in his eye, sacrificing himself for the needs of others, and letting the Holy Spirit determine the results. Until every Wesleyan, clergy or laity, young or old, great or small, sees himself or herself as a priest offering the sacrifice of grace, the vision of a global parish is a fleeting fantasy.

Authorized by Experience

To assume that the world is our parish might still smack of arrogance. Paul confronted that question by telling us that *he was authorized by experience to take the gospel to the Gentiles.* He wrote, "I will not venture to speak of anything except what Christ has accomplished through me" (Romans 15:18). Paul was saying that he would not preach above or beyond his experience.

What a threat to our witness! If we followed Paul's principle, many of us would have little to say about the gospel. Too many witnesses to the gospel, both clergy and laity, assume that we can separate speaking biblical truth from the way we live. Yet, Paul's principle is the one we should follow.

The story is told about a British preacher who got on a local bus, needed change to pay his fare, and when seated, discovered that the driver had given him the wrong change. Because the error was in his favor, he debated whether or not to give it back to the driver. *After all,* he thought, *I have often been shortchanged.*

Finally, when he arrived at his stop, he told the driver, "You made a mistake and gave me the wrong change."

The driver answered, "It was no mistake. I heard your sermon on Sunday morning, and I wanted to find out if you really mean what you say."

Each of us has had a similar experience. When we take the name "Christian," "Wesleyan," or "Evangelical," we invite the scrutiny of those who expect us to live up to our name.

Our 21st-Century World Parish

In past eras, Wesleyans have moved as evangelists and missionaries from the security and stature of a home base into uncharted territories. As glorious as our past history of missionary ventures may be, we must confess that our spiritual forebears were working on the assumption of a divided world, part Christian and part pagan.

Our view of the world must change in the 21st century. *We can no longer rest in the luxury of a culture undergirded by the moral concepts of our Christian faith.* Although there is still the residual evidence of a Christian culture in North

America, secular attitudes dominate us, selfish motives drive us, and sinful actions define us.

Racial, ethnic, economic, and religious diversity in the 21st century will further change the character of our global parish. Colors blend, cultures mix, and creeds clash in our urban world. Every expert of demographics is predicting that this is the dominant picture of our nation in the 21st century.

How do we witness in this changing global parish? We must still be compelled by conviction, commissioned by grace, and authorized by experience as we follow the strategy of the Holy Spirit into the world. However, our outlook must change.

First, we must recognize that every nation is a mission field. To divide the world into home and foreign fields or into local church and global ministries is no longer real nor right. With this division comes the superior attitude of which Christians have been accused by critics of world missions. Although the criticism is unfair, we must confess the tendency to see ourselves as the majority addressing the minority, the educated teaching the ignorant, the cultured tolerating the uncouth, the rich giving to the poor, and the Christian helping the heathen. As brutal as this may sound, it is confirmed in the world assemblies of our churches. By fact or inference, white Westerners still tend to dominate the leadership, determine the agenda, and are solicitous of their non-Western brothers and sisters.

Our world parish in the 21st century will dispel that divided world, and with it will go every shred of our superiority. Leading the way is the indisputable fact that the Lord has chosen the underdeveloped nations south of the equator as the place where His Spirit is being poured out on all flesh. In the West, we *pray* for spiritual awakening; in the South, they are *experiencing* it. The East and the Far East are not far behind. Revivals have come to Russia and China while we await the evidence that will change our culture.

Putting these facts together, North America is as much a mission field as any nation in the world. Contextualization and cross-culture ministries are no longer concepts that we learn to apply overseas. In our changing world parish, they are essential tools of our witness to a neighbor across the street or a native across the world.

If every nation is a mission field, a second mind-changing fact comes forward: *We must equip every congregation to be a sending society.* Few churches see themselves as mission outposts in a pagan society. We leave that definition to institutionalized missions in urban, rural, and ethnic ghettoes. No more. When we shape the definition of a mature church in the 21st century, we must go beyond the worthy goals of a soul-winning church, a disciple-making ministry, and even a church-planting congregation. We must begin to think about becoming a sending church. Nothing is wrong with the other goals, except that they tend to be geared to a similar culture of persons who have some background in the faith and are socially compatible with us. A sending church implies a mixed culture among persons who are ignorant of the faith and whose social differences make us uncomfortable.

Again, overseas congregations where the Spirit of God has graciously moved in spiritual awakening have become models for sending churches. From these churches, we need to learn how to enlarge our vision and equip our people in order to qualify as sending congregations ready to serve in our changing world parish.

If every nation is a mission field and every congregation is a sending society, then a third fact naturally follows: *Every member must be a missionary.* Certainly, this is not the idea of membership that most Christians in our churches have at the present time. At the least, we expect the church to serve us. At the most, we are willing to sacrifice some discretionary time to teach a class, attend a Bible study, share a witness, or take a missions trip. If every member becomes a missionary, however, all of these dimensions change. Simply make a list of the expectations that we have for our missionaries, and we will see the radical change in expectations for church members. We would expect our people to see themselves in full-time Christian ministry, whatever their profession might be; making sacrifices of time, money, and prestige in order to make the name of Christ known; learning how to communicate across cultural lines; demonstrating the meaning of holy living in a pagan environment; and giving themselves in love to needy people whom they do not know or understand. As radical as this may seem, it is the first step in revolutionizing the church, regaining our momentum, and revitalizing our spirit.

Wesleyans have the historical precedent to lead the way into our world parish of the 21st century. Once again, the challenge is out. Will Wesleyans take the risk of showing the way of witness in our 21st-century global parish? If so, every nation must be our mission field, every congregation must be a sending society, and every member must be a missionary.

Notes:

1. *The Complete Works of John Wesley,* vol. 1 (Albany, Oreg.: AGES Software, 1997), 227.
2. Wesley, vol. 1, 210.
3. Wesley, vol. 1, 227.
4. Wesley, vol. 1, 228.

Scriptures Cited: Mark 1:37-38; Romans 15:16, 18, 20; Galatians 5:6; Philippians 4:18

About the Author: This chapter has been excerpted from *What a Time to Be Wesleyan!* (Kansas City: Beacon Hill Press of Kansas City, 1999) by David McKenna. Used by permission, all rights reserved. Dr. McKenna, a noted scholar and public speaker, is a former president of Asbury Theological Seminary in Wilmore, Kentucky.

CHAPTER 6

One Size Doesn't Fit All
by Everett Leadingham

SOMEONE CAME up to D. L. Moody one day and said, "I don't like your method of evangelism."

Moody asked, "What is your method?"

"I really don't have one. I just don't like yours," the person replied.

"Well," Moody responded, "I like my way of doing it better than your way of *not* doing it!"

The person who confronted D. L. Moody could have been almost anyone, because it has been estimated that 95 percent of all church members have never led a person to Christ.* Perhaps one reason for this is that most Christians do not think of themselves as having the gift of evangelism. Often their view of what it means to share the gospel with others is rather narrow. Say the word "witness" to a Christian, and he or she will most likely think of people who buttonhole unwilling listeners and explain four spiritual laws to them.

However, that stereotypical method need not be the way everyone witnesses to faith in Christ. In this chapter we will broaden our horizons by looking at five different ways to cultivate evangelistic relationships.

Some Things in Common

Before we get into each of the five different ways, let's review some ideas, maybe misconceptions, that apply to evangelism across the board.

Conversion does not usually occur with only one encounter.

55

One study coming from church growth literature discovered 5.7 hearings of the gospel are necessary before a person accepts the Lord and stays true to God. On the other hand, the person who starts his or her life with Christ but does not continue has often heard the gospel only 2.3 times.

Though our perception may be that people usually respond the first time they hear the glorious Good News, those dramatic conversions are preceded by several encounters with different Christians. Every new creature in Christ is the result of a cooperative effort. As Paul pointed out, "I planted the seed, Apollos watered it, but God made it grow" (1 Corinthians 3:6).

Factors affecting the likelihood of persons accepting Christ may not be what we imagine them to be. While age affects the likelihood of one becoming a Christian, it is not as great a factor as educational level. Only 66 percent of college graduates believe in Jesus. Persons in college are far more likely to question traditional beliefs about Jesus, even if those traditional beliefs are uninformed.

Still, education does not always directly correlate to skepticism about certain religious issues. Interestingly enough, people with less than a high school education are more skeptical about there being life after death than are college graduates. And race somewhat affects the likelihood of persons believing in God. Eighty-two percent of white Americans believe that Jesus is God, while African-Americans weigh in at 94 percent. Hispanics fall in between at 89 percent.

Progress may not be apparent in every evangelistic effort. Because we are dependent upon the Holy Spirit's work and the other person's willingness, we may go away empty-handed and feel we have failed. The person simply may not be ready. We may be only planting the seed or watering. It is often hard to tell.

Resistance, even outright rejection, is sometimes part of the process of witnessing. We need to be aware of this and be prepared to deal with it when it happens. Many, for very personal reasons unknown to us, will resist any effort to get them involved in spiritual conversations. Also, we must keep in mind that as we try to witness to the truth of Christ, some will reject and may even persecute or ridicule us. As Paul reminded us, "Our struggle is not against flesh and blood, but against the rulers, against the authorities, against the powers of this dark world and against the spiritual forces of evil in the heavenly realms" (Ephesians 6:12). Evangelism is telling the "good news" *over against* the "bad news." It is attempting to bring light to darkness, and those in the darkness may resist and reject such efforts.

Every Christian has at least one thing to share—his or her own story of faith. Just as none of our conversion stories is like anyone else's (because it is our personal history), so we need not all use the same method to share our faith. Our task is to find the gifts and desires God has placed in us and use them to tell others about Jesus.

With these ideas common to all evangelistic methods in mind, let's look at five different ways to approach spiritual relationships with others.

Everyone Wants a Friend

Many people overlook friendship as a means of evangelism. Yet, this may be the "easiest" method of all because nearly every human being wants and needs a friend. What would make a better bridge to introducing someone to our best Friend than genuine Christian friendship?

On the surface, friendship may not seem to be evangelism because it involves doing things that even non-Christians can do. Yet for a Christian, the motivation behind friendship is sharing the gospel. In the midst of a friendly relationship, opportunities will arise to answer questions about faith. If we are authentic Christians, our friends cannot help but notice the impact our faith has on our lives. Their curiosity will cause them to ask, and we can tell them about Jesus. That is evangelism!

In the parable about the sheep and the goats (Matthew 25:31-45), Jesus described some activities that can be seen as acts of friendship. Sharing a meal with a hungry person meets physical and social needs. Talking over soft drinks or coffee helps friends get to know one another. Nothing is more heartwarming than being invited into friendship by a kind stranger. The Christian who visits another person who is in some kind of trouble, especially when others are avoiding the person in pain, is indeed a true friend. Always the motivation behind such friendly behavior is thankfulness for what God in Christ has done for us.

There is one thing we need to keep in mind if we feel called to friendship evangelism. Christians are in for the long haul. That means we must be willing to continue friendship at two different critical points. After our friend becomes a believer in Jesus, we will not drop him or her and move on to another "target." Instead, we will continue our friendship, guiding the new believer to assimilate into our faith community. On the other hand, if our friend tells us not to talk about religion anymore, we will respect his or her wishes but continue all the other aspects of the friendship. We will wait patiently for him or her to be open again to spiritual conversations.

Y'all Come!

Another avenue of evangelism that many Christians do not think of as witnessing is what we might call "the gift of invitation." Let's face it, some of us are better at advertising, and can be the ones who invite persons to church events, and ultimately to Christ.

There are many ways witnessing as "advertising" can be done. Here are just a few examples. You can probably think of others as well.

- Inviting coworkers to church services, particularly at special seasons of the year when church attendance by non-churchgoers is considered "OK"—Christmas and Easter.
- Providing transportation to church for those who could not attend otherwise. This is an action that says, "I care

enough about you to put forth extra effort." That is a very inviting and appreciated implied statement.

☐ Get involved with actual advertisement pieces for the church. You might get involved in the graphics and help create the material. Or you might help distribute the invitations door-to-door in your neighborhood. (A couple years ago, our local congregation was involved in hanging copies of the *JESUS* film video on our neighbors' doors. It did not involve knocking on any doors, for the printed materials in the bag were all the invitation we needed to express.)

☐ In casual conversations, another subtle but inviting action is to talk positively about the good things that happen at church. This might spark someone's curiosity enough that he or she would attend "just to see what's going on."

☐ Of course, another aspect of invitation evangelism can occur inside the church building itself. The greeters at the door set a welcoming tone, which invites visitors to come in and share the church's experience.

A distinguishing feature of invitation as a form of evangelism is the focus on what persons are being invited to attend. All of the activities of the church in some way or another reflect the message of Christ. Worship services are perhaps the most obvious times when God is publicly worshiped. However, inviting someone to a Sunday School class is extending an invitation to learn about the Bible and the God of the Bible. Home Bible studies are another place we can invite persons to learn about the Scriptures and our Christian faith.

Other special events are planned for the main purpose of inviting unchurched persons. These can include concerts by Christian musicians, dinner-dramas that exhibit Christian values, and seminars with special speakers. One of the most important invitations in our tradition is asking persons to attend special revival meetings where they will hear an evangelist share the gospel.

Easing the Suffering

It is true that nearly everyone wants or needs a friend. It is also a pleasant thing to be invited to share a good experience with friends. However, many persons have desperate needs in their lives, and these are opportunities for evangelism for some Christians.

This aspect of evangelism is often labeled "compassionate ministry." Others call them "acts of mercy." Whatever name we use, compassion is at the very heart of evangelism. In three of the four Gospels—Matthew, Mark, and Luke—the words "Jesus" and "compassion" are linked. In the parable of the sheep and the goats mentioned earlier, Jesus was describing acts of compassion. He said, in relation to their importance, "'Whatever you did for one of the least of these brothers of mine, you did for me'" (Matthew 25:40).

Though non-Christians can and do perform "acts of mercy," Christians' actions differ from mere social action. A Christian relieves suffering as an act of evangelism to intentionally follow Jesus' words and example. Medical missionaries are an example of this. Their visible "job" is to provide medical treatment, but their reason for doing this is to spread the gospel of Jesus Christ.

The apostle Paul recognized the source and purpose of compassion in this adoration: "Praise be to the God and Father of our Lord Jesus Christ, the Father of compassion and the God of all comfort, who comforts us in all our troubles, so that we can comfort those in any trouble with the comfort we ourselves have received from God" (2 Corinthians 1:3-4). James was also direct in his word to Christians about compassion: "Religion that God our Father accepts as pure and faultless is this: to look after orphans and widows in their distress and to keep oneself from being polluted by the world" (James 1:27).

Peter summed up the proper attitude for a Christian who engages in compassionate ministry as evangelism, an attitude that sets Christian acts of mercy apart from secular efforts. *"In your hearts set apart Christ as Lord. Always be prepared to give an answer* to everyone who asks you to give the reason for the hope that you have. But do this with gentleness and respect, keeping a clear conscience, so that those who speak maliciously against your good behavior in Christ may be ashamed of their slander. *It is better, if it is God's will, to suffer for doing good than for doing evil"* (1 Peter 3:15-17, emphasis added).

Let MeTellYou Some Good News!

Next, we arrive at the method most people associate with evangelism—confrontation and persuasion. Another name for this is "personal evangelism." Some Christians will be called to this ministry, though obviously not everyone is. Though this method requires a person to be somewhat outgoing to confront people about the Lord, even shy persons prepared by training and empowered by the Holy Spirit can engage in this kind of direct evangelism.

The key to being effective in personal evangelism is preparation. Most of this is dealt with in training classes. A personal evangelist needs to have a good grasp of some basic theology—such as who God is, who Jesus was, how the Holy Spirit is present in the world today, and what the purpose of the Church is. He or she should also have understandable working definitions of important terms like "forgiveness," "mercy," "grace," "salvation," and "holiness."

In addition, a personal evangelist must get ready to witness by learning about the persons to whom he or she will be speaking. In general terms, certain groups share certain characteristics. We will have more specific things to say in this regard in later chapters. When it comes to specific individuals, the personal evangelist needs to be trained to find out important information about the person with whom he or she will share the gospel. What is this person's circumstance in life? What does he or she believe about God and the Church? What does he or she want out of life? Is he or she ready to hear the truth and accept Christ as Savior?

Finally, the personal evangelist must be equipped to share the gospel in a clear and concise way. Such persons learn to give the basics of the gospel in short presentations. They will have 5-minute, 10-minute, and 20-minute presentations memorized so they can share clearly while adapting to the circumstances. These presentations also make use of specially marked Bible passages that can be found easily at the appropriate moment. In addition, some personal evangelists use printed material to guide their presentation (such as the Four Spiritual Laws booklet).

Attitudes are key to effective personal evangelism. It is important to remember that it is the work of the Holy Spirit to convince a person of his or her sin. It is the person's free will to make the decision to accept Christ. As evangelists, we are simply willing tools God uses to do *His* work in people's lives.

Keeping that in mind will help us to remember that it is our humble privilege to be a part of God's redemption of fallen humanity. Seeing others as God sees them will allow us to confront them without being judgmental or feeling spiritually superior. As personal evangelists, we are God's servants. We must always remember our place in the divine scheme of things.

Here's the Reason Why

Finally, we turn to the most specialized form of evangelism—explaining to a larger audience why we believe what we do. Sometimes this is called "intellectual evangelism" because it involves writing, preaching, or teaching ministry. It is also called "apologetics" (not because we're sorry that we're Christians, but coming from the Greek word meaning "to defend").

This type of evangelism can be done by laypersons or those with ministerial credentials. Either way, this takes specialized education and training. Persons called to defend Christianity intellectually need to study the Bible, theology, philosophy, psychology, and creative arts to be prepared to share the gospel with the world.

Part of the task of intellectual evangelism is finding ways to deliver the gospel to wide audiences outside the Church. These people become teachers, reporters, playwrights, poets, and writers. Another aspect of this type of evangelism is equipping local churches with materials for understanding the Christian faith and spreading the gospel. A few of the intellectual evangelists are called to do research so they can understand cultural ideas and what resources congregations need to minister in their cultural context.

Making a Faithful Choice

The apostle Paul posed a series of important questions to the Christians at Rome. These same questions pose an evangelism challenge to us today. "'Anyone who calls on the name of the Lord will be saved.' But how can they call on him to save them unless they believe in him? And how can they believe in him if they have never heard about him? And how can they hear about him unless someone tells them?" (Romans 10:13-14, NLT).

Evangelism is not an option for those whose lives have been transformed in Christ. The only option is which method of evangelism we will embrace. We need to carefully consider our gifts and desires in order to find the style of evangelism that best fits who God has created us to be.

We do not want to be like the person who confronted D. L. Moody. We want to move out of the dismal percentage of those who have never led anyone to Christ. There are many ways to do evangelism. We need only to pick one and "just do it."

*Paul Lee Tan, *Encyclopedia of 7,700 Illustrations* (Rockville, Md.: Assurance Publishers, 1984), 1316.

Scriptures Cited: Matthew 25:31-45; Romans 10:13-14; 1 Corinthians 3:6; 2 Corinthians 1:3-4; Ephesians 6:12; James 1:27; 1 Peter 3:15-17

About the Author: Dr. Everett Leadingham is the editor of the Dialog Series for the Church of the Nazarene, Kansas City, Missouri. Portions of this chapter were adapted from an unpublished manuscript by Lyle Pointer and Brint Montgomery. Used by permission; all rights reserved.

CHAPTER 7

Pluralism: Getting Along with Everyone

by Everett Leadingham

IT WAS A SIMPLE wedding. She had on a gingham dress, and he wore buckskin breeches. They were in love, and that's all that mattered to them.

The next morning, they set out from the port city of Baltimore and headed west. They carried everything they owned with them. They had a few dishes and eating utensils, some tools for working with wood, a couple of months' supply of food, a few chickens, and a cow. They carried all their goods in a wagon pulled by a horse, with the cow walking along behind.

The year was 1792. For the next four long weeks, they made their way across the Appalachian Mountains and the Ohio River Valley. They endured soaking rains and searing sunshine. Finally, they reached their destination, just a few miles north of Marietta, Ohio.

There, he set about clearing a small patch of the forest and building a rough cabin. She helped her husband build the shelter and then turn it into a cozy home the best she could. Next they built a small barn to house the horse, cow, and chickens. As the snows of their first winter on the frontier set in, they huddled around the fireplace and dreamed of their future together.

This pioneer couple was tough and independent. They had to be—not many other people were around. Less than 150 people lived in the newly founded town of Marietta.

The other settlers were busy clearing their own land and building their own shelters.

This unnamed pair of newlyweds may seem insignificant, though they could have been my great-great-grandparents. Yet, they were at the beginning of a movement that has mutated into a philosophy permeating our culture today. In this chapter, we will track the progression of this outlook, which appears in various forms and presents formidable challenges to our evangelism efforts.

The Story Repeated

The story of this young couple setting out to build their future on the frontier was repeated over and over as Americans moved further west. The rigors of such experiences developed a breed of hardy, self-sufficient individuals. In those days, it was the individual against the elements of nature, including the sometimes-hostile people who were already living in the "wide open" land.

Rugged individualism became an honored characteristic among those who carved civilization out of the American wilderness. It was necessary for survival in those conditions. However, individualism has remained ingrained in our culture, long after its usefulness for survival has passed. In fact, the concept has changed into something that works against the fabric of community.

Why?

One reason might be that people have misunderstood freedom. Many people think of freedom as their ability to do whatever they want, regardless of consequences or effect on other people. Such a selfish understanding of freedom causes behaviors that undermine society rather than build it up.

For example, some people think that freedom means they have every right to use whatever drugs they want or sleep with whomever they want. They have little or no regard for how those behaviors destroy their bodies, their families, and their lives.

Too many people have forgotten that freedom is an opportunity to choose to do what is right. This is truly a free choice. We can either choose to do the moral and godly things or we can elect to indulge in sinful behaviors that lead to destruction and death. If we choose God's way, we have true freedom to experience all the good things God intends for us. The apostle Paul explained it like this to those early believers who had chosen to follow Christ: "Now you are free from the power of sin. . . . Now you do those things that lead to holiness and result in eternal life" (Romans 6:22, NLT).

We're Still Individuals

It is true that each of us is an individual, a unique person. Looks, talents, and experiences are different for each of us. Everything we know about life, we know from our personal perspective.

In today's concept of individualism, personal perspective is raised to an unwarranted importance. Everything is considered on the basis of what it means to the individual. "What does this mean *to me?*" becomes the standard question. In effect, "I" becomes the highest authority on every matter. This is usually an emotional judgment: how it makes me *feel* determines whether I *think* it is important or not.

It is only a short step to the consequence of such individualistic thinking. Persons who are this self-centered can easily believe that absolute truth doesn't exist. They will say, "My truth differs from your truth. Truth is what each person thinks it is."

Thus, individualism sets the solitary person up as the ultimate authority on every subject. The Bible no longer has anything relevant to say (so individualism thinks). God is no longer the ruler of the universe. Only what the individual human being deems true or existent is important.

How can society exist if every one of us is entitled to decide what is true or worthwhile? Won't our perspectives clash and turn everything into chaos?

Enter Pluralism

Before we turn to the specific problems pluralism causes in our evangelistic efforts, let's look at how it shows up in typical conversations. Basically, pluralism is expressed in two forms. One is diversity. This is simply the recognition that we are not the same. We are different persons, each unique in our own way. Christianity embraces this. We believe that there is a great deal of variety in the mind and heart of the Creator. God embraces a wide diversity of ethnicity, intellectual capacities, thought processes, and approaches to life. People look at life through different filters. Christianity appreciates diversity and works with it.

There is another form of pluralism that we might call "dogmatic." This position says that being different is absolute and unchangeable. For us to ask someone to change and look at things differently is abominable because we are asking him or her to surrender the things that make his or her identity unique.

Pluralism is the basis for a group of people who are vastly different from each other to try to live together without chaos reigning. Individualism needs dogmatic pluralism so that everyone has the right to be whoever he or she is, regardless of how that affects anyone else.

This latter version of pluralism comes to the foreground most clearly in religious matters. The ideas are ingrained in secular culture and even creep into Christian circles. With their commitment to unchangeable diversity, pluralism and individualism make it hard to get people to listen to the idea of being changed by Christ. Respect for diversity sometimes causes Christians to be hesitant to talk to anyone about the possibility of changing. "Why can't we all just get along?" becomes the plaintive cry of Christians and non-Christians alike.

Even when we Christians find the balance between asking a person to change into a believer in Christ without giving up his or her ethnic and cultural uniqueness, another "ism" rears its ugly head to make our evangelistic task difficult. The term is "postmodernism." Combining both individualism and pluralism, this word describes how we have moved past the "modern" view of proving truth by observation and logical thinking.

Postmodernism says there is no absolute truth; every individual decides his or her own truth. And more important, postmodernism is hostile to *moral* truth. That is, nothing is right or wrong except what a person decides is right or wrong for himself or herself.

What We've Heard

If we listen closely, we will hear people around us saying various things that are accepted as true statements in our culture. Yet, they are really reflections of the individualism and pluralism that pervade the current times. Sometimes we might even notice similar statements coming from our own mouths, for the Church is surrounded and invaded by these ideas too.

How often have we heard someone say, "There is good in everyone"? That is probably true, up to a certain point. Most people, outside the truly heinous criminals, probably do have several good characteristics. However, this statement becomes a hindrance for evangelism when what it really means is that people are naturally good and don't need to change. People begin to think that their good characteristics will outweigh any bad they do, and that will make them acceptable to God.

The Bible has a different view. The apostle Paul, in comparing the Gentiles and the Israelites, makes the point that still applies to us. The Gentiles have obtained God's righteousness by faith. The Israelites, though they have pursued the law diligently, have not obtained that righteousness. "Why not? Because they pursued it not by faith but as if it were by works" (Romans 9:32). They made an effort to get the good to outweigh the bad in a person. However, God provided a different way. "For it is by grace you have been saved, through faith . . . not by works, so that no one can boast" (Ephesians 2:8-9).

Often people counter those who believe what the Bible says about sin by stating, "God is too loving to send anyone to hell." Of course, it is painful for us to even imagine anyone suffering eternal torment, but the Bible is clear that God will punish those who reject Him. To the ones who have raised individualism to the highest authority, the Bible says, "Because of your stubbornness and your unrepentant heart, you are storing up wrath against yourself for the day of God's wrath, when his righteous judgment will be revealed. God 'will give to each person according to what he has done.' . . . For those who are self-seeking and who reject the truth and follow evil, there will be wrath and anger. . . . For God does not show favoritism" (Romans 2:5-6, 8, 11).

In the conversation with evangelism, pluralism sometimes moves to another, more distancing position. How familiar is this sentiment? "No one has the right to tell anyone else how to live his or her life. We each have to do what's best for ourselves." Granted, we should always do what is best. However, it should be the good God intended, not merely following the selfish desires we have. Helping the world to see what God intended for human beings is the evangelical Christian task, and that involves telling others how God intends for us to live.

Resistance to our witnessing to God's plan will often come in this dismissive statement: "That's OK for you, but it doesn't work for me." This is individualism saying, "Don't try to change me; I'm fine the way I am."

Are we all free to choose our own way to God? Are there many different but equally good "paths up the mountain"? Evangelical Christians do not believe so. Jesus said, "I am the way and the truth and the life. No one comes to the Father except through me" (John 14:6). Peter wrote in the culture of his day, "The Lord . . . is patient with you, not wanting anyone to perish, but *everyone* to come to repentance" (2 Peter 3:9, emphasis added). And Christians are compelled to share the Good News by verses such as this: "Without holiness no one will see the Lord. See to it that *no one* misses the *grace* of God" (Hebrews 12:14-15, emphasis added).

Finally, firmly entrenched pluralism will boldly declare, "There is no truth." In attempting to reject all truth, this statement is logically false, for it claims that what it is—a statement of truth—does not exist. Another way an evangelical can show the logical implosion of such a declaration is by looking at how people use language. Parents teach their children to speak about the world and its events. Children are able to pick-up the rules and vocabulary of their parents' language. This could not be done if language were an arbitrary collection of noises, without any truthful tie to the existent world. Adults often argue about the meaning of words and about subtle shades of distinctions in meanings, but this is hardly evidence to conclude that words cannot carry truthful content about the present or past, cannot refer to what we had for supper last night, or to what a man had to say while dying on a cross 2,000 years ago.

The Truth of Christianity

The current climate in our culture makes evangelism difficult, but not impossible. We need to be aware of the ideas that permeate so much of the thinking today, so that we can be ready to separate truth from fiction.

The truth of Christianity is not relative, that is, it does not change depending on how one person or another views it differently. Rather, certain things are true, regardless of human opinion about them.

The Bible is clear that "God is love" (1 John 4:16). And because of God's love, He sent His only Son Jesus into the world to redeem the world from the prison of sin. Anyone who believes that Jesus is the Son of God will have eternal life, a free gift of grace from God (see John 3:16 and Galatians 4:4-5).

Salvation is not a relative thing. We *know* the truth of God through Christ. We believe the truth, and we tell others about it. Still, the apostle John challenges us to go even further. "Let us stop just saying we love each other; let us really show it by our actions. It is by our actions that we know we are *living in the truth*" (1 John 3:18-19, NLT, emphasis added). Unbelievers' opinions will not water down the truth either. As Paul declared, "What if some did not have faith? Will their lack of faith nullify God's faithfulness? Not at all! Let God be true, and every man a liar" (Romans 3:3-4).

Salvation is not a "do-it-yourself" project, as pluralistic ideas would lead us to believe. The days of rugged individualism are over. It served us well in pioneer days, but it pulls us apart in the present age. No one can find the way to salvation simply by following his or her own individual path. Now is the time for us to draw together as a community that believes in Jesus Christ as "the way and the truth and the life" (John 14:6).

And today is the day to invite everyone—regardless of their differences or their misunderstanding of truth—to join us.

Scriptures Cited: John 3:16; 14:6; Romans 2:5-6, 8, 11; 3:3-4; 6:22; 9:32; Galatians 4:4-5; Ephesians 2:8-9; Hebrews 12:14-15; 2 Peter 3:9; 1 John 3:18-19; 4:16

About the Author: Dr. Everett Leadingham is the editor of the Dialog Series for the Church of the Nazarene, Kansas City, Missouri. Portions of this chapter were adapted from an unpublished manuscript by Lyle Pointer and Brint Montgomery. Used by permission; all rights reserved.

CHAPTER 8

The Challenge to "Prove It!"

by Everett Leadingham

SOMETIMES IT SEEMS to me that we have a saying for almost everything. No matter what the situation, we can find a well-worn phrase to use in talking about it. These adages come from lots of different sources—poets, bumper stickers, songs, and even the Bible.

Here are some examples of what I mean:

When parents want to warn their children about hanging out with the wrong crowd, they can use this saying: "Birds of a feather flock together." In other words, if you hang with those bad kids, you will be seen as a bad person.

When we want to admonish someone to be careful with his or her investments, this proverb comes in handy: "A fool and his money are soon parted."

Nearly everyone has been behind a car with a bumper sticker that announces: "The one who dies with the most toys wins."

The romantic ones among us are quick to quote: "Love makes the world go 'round."

And it is not unusual to see someone lean back contentedly in his or her chair and quote: "God's in His heaven; all's right with the world."

Though there are thousands more sayings we can—and do—quote, perhaps the most difficult one for evangelism is: "Seeing is believing." Those who live by this adage have a hard time believing in anything they cannot see or touch.

This particular way of looking at the world was present even in New Testament times. The disciple Thomas missed the Easter Sunday evening service in which Jesus appeared to the other disciples (see John 20:19). When the others shared with Thomas their joyous experience of seeing the Lord, he retreated to the "I need proof" position. "Unless I see the nail marks in his hands and put my finger where the nails were, and put my hand into his side, I will not believe it," he told them (John 20:24).

When his turn came to encounter the Risen Lord, Thomas did not actually need the proof he had suggested. Instead of putting his finger in the nail holes or poking his hand into Jesus' split side, "Thomas said to him, 'My Lord and my God!'" (20:28). Nevertheless, the damage was done. To this day, people refer to this disciple as "doubting Thomas." And far too many people still imitate him when it comes to spiritual matters, saying, "I need proof."

Believing what we can see or touch is a natural human trait. Yet, most people also have faith in things which cannot be seen or touched. The problem for evangelism arises from those persons who insist on the same kind of proof for spiritual matters as scientific ones.

In this chapter, we want to examine this need for proof and how Christians can respond evangelistically to it.

The Rise of Science

Let's take a quick little tour through history, since everything has come to us down the halls of time.

For the first 400 years of the Christian church, the Roman Empire was still in power. In A.D. 312 the emperor Constantine became a Christian, and declared Christianity to be the official religion of the Roman Empire. Around A.D. 400 the empire's might waned, especially in the far reaches of Europe.

The next 1,000 years or so we call "the Middle Ages." This period did without the luxuries previously provided by the Romans—especially safety and education. Sometimes these years are called "the Dark Ages" for many chaotic battles were fought and people were ignorant and superstitious.

Around A.D. 1400 things began to change. A renewed interest in learning, art, and religion arose. This period has been labeled "the Renaissance" (or "rebirth"). Shortly after this renewal began, the age of scientific discovery started.

With this scientific age came a shift in thinking that has greatly impacted our present culture. Experiments and logic became the only criteria by which something was to be believed. Belief based on unprovable ideas moved to a backseat. As time went on, science gained the upper hand in explaining the natural world, while explanations based on God waned.

That brings us to three big words that we need to understand as we think about evangelizing persons who are steeped in the scientific way of thinking. The first one we have already been using—*scientific.* In its strictest sense, *scientific* applies to only those facts which can be verified in repeatable experiments. In other words, if multiple scientists can produce the same results independent of each other, then the facts are considered true scientifically.

The second related word is *empiricism.* This is the "five-dollar" version used by those educated persons whose beliefs are based only on scientific proof. It simply means relying on observation and experiments, that is, relying on scientific research.

The third word that comes up often in a discussion such as this is *rationalism.* Webster explains it this way: "a theory that reason [the thinking process] is in itself a source of knowledge superior to and independent of sense perception."* Rationalism takes a little different spin on "seeing is believing" and says, "thinking is believing." Persons who rely heavily on rationality believe they can think their way through any problem. And they demand that everything be logically consistent, a perspective that keeps many from accepting Christianity or believing the Bible.

Science and Evangelism

Since the 1960s, public education in Western culture has been based on the assumed superiority of science and technology. This has resulted in a philosophy that permeates many people's thinking: If science and technology cannot solve a problem, it is unsolvable.

Granted, many advances have been made that have made our lives healthier and easier. However, one casualty of this rise of belief in science has been religious belief. In this age, how do we tell people about the truth of things that cannot be proven in a laboratory? That is the challenge of evangelization to the many who say, "I need proof!"

What kind of questions will these persons, who have raised reasoning and science to the most important place in their belief system, ask? The most basic question, of course, would be: "Does God exist?" Along with that, they would ask, "Is the Bible true?" From that springs a list of pertinent questions, with which evangelicals must deal.

- Did a man named Jesus live and die 2,000 years ago?
- Did He come back to life?
- Do His death and resurrection have anything to do with me?
- How can you *prove* that any of this is true?

Ultimately, it boils down to a question of authority for the person to whom we are talking. What would he or she consider to be sufficient evidence to get him or her to believe in Jesus?

Sometimes even proof a person asks for will not work. One evangelist was working with such a person, whom we can call Larry. Larry said that if God arranged circumstances in a certain way, he would believe in Jesus. God did arrange things the way he had asked. Yet, Larry still did not accept Christ. When the evangelist confronted Larry about the fact that God had provided the very proof he had demanded, Larry simply shrugged it off as coincidence. The evangelist learned that although Larry had appeared to be open to proof, in reality his rationality was just a smokescreen for not wanting to become a Christian. The reasons behind such a position are not readily apparent to us as we share the gospel.

Two Sides to Every Question

Conversations between evangelicals and persons of a scientific mind often revolve around the physical world. Scientific experiments are most often concerned with what can be observed in nature. Nevertheless, it is always possible for two people to interpret the same set of facts in different ways. Let's take a look at two types of "data" from which Christians and scientists often draw different conclusions, yet can be useful in our evangelistic task.

First, let's consider *general revelation.* Christians consider that nature is God's handiwork and tells us something about the Creator. Most Christians believe as the apostle Paul did when he wrote: "Since the creation of the world God's invisible qualities—his eternal power and divine nature—have been clearly seen, being understood from what has been made" (Romans 1:20). In other words, God has revealed something about himself in a general way, and we can see this when we examine the creation.

Scientists often draw a different conclusion when they observe nature. They give nature itself the creative power as it changes and evolves over long periods of time. They do not readily see the variety and consistency of nature as proof of God's existence.

In our spiritual conversations with people who believe as many scientists do, we may be able to help them see the data in a different way. Since they believe that science is the key to understanding nature, perhaps they can come to see that science can also be the key to understanding God by understanding His creation.

For example, the moon remains at a consistent distance that has varying positive effects on the earth, such as gravity. For the moon to get out of its orbit would cause the disintegration of the earth. The same can be said of the sun. Since those destructive things do not happen, we can conclude that we live in a rational universe. Without such predictability, science would yield no logical knowledge. It is not a very long step, then, to realize that a rational mind created the universe we observe.

The second area for us to consider is *special revelation*. Here we move from general and observable facts to the authority of the Bible. Special revelation refers to the witness of God's Spirit in the Bible. The nature of humanity reflects the Creator. Being made in the image of God means that the teachings of God are compatible with what we are like and what we should become.

For Christians, the Bible is the highest authority in matters of faith. For non-Christians, especially those who demand scientific proof, the Bible is not an authority. The purpose of spiritual conversations with such persons is to get them to accept biblical authority on some level.

The most effective way to use the Bible is in light of how it is accepted by the one to whom we are witnessing. We need to find out what he or she thinks of the Bible. The way to find out is simply to use the Bible. If the person accepts it, fine. If he or she discredits it, we must be willing to explore his or her specific disagreements. Once we know the particular objections, we can decide how to use the Bible as an authority, perhaps only addressing the main themes of the Bible or maybe moving to other avenues.

Wesleyan-Holiness Christians utilize additional resources to help us understand Scripture. This is a practice we have inherited from our spiritual forebear John Wesley. Skeptical scientific minds may embrace these additional resources more easily than the Bible itself.

To understand any scripture, Wesleyans ask three questions. (1) How has Christian tradition interpreted the passage over the centuries? (2) What does our God-given reasoning ability tell us? And (3) is this truth borne out in our experience?

The "I need proof" folks use four similar processes in determining the truth of their facts. Rather than the Bible, their authorities extend back to only those experiments upon which their present work builds. Traditional interpretations for them are those scientists who have proven certain theories. Their experience is limited to the verifiable experiments in the laboratory. And reason for scientists is the ability to make sense of the data and pull the proof together into a coherent theory.

The Christian witness who understands how the scientific mind thinks may be able to help the non-Christian open up to the possibility of other authority than what we can simply observe. The aim of this type of evangelism is to level the playing field so that faith claims both for and against God can be considered. Then the evangelist can eliminate false biases, such as Christianity is irrational and thus unacceptable.

One way to open the door to thinking about other authorities might be to ask the person if his or her spouse (or parents) loves him or her. If the response is positive, ask, "How do you know?" He or she will probably respond in terms of behaviors observed in the other person that he or she interprets as proving love. When he or she realizes that the interpreted actions are a faith statement about love, he or she might be open to taking another look at the general revelation of God in nature and special revelation in the Bible.

The Challenge Remains

Though for discussion purposes it is easier to clearly differentiate between scientific and Christian positions, reality is not that clear. There is always a mixture present. Even in the most rational person, there are certain aspects he or she more or less accepts on faith. And in the most devout Christian, there may be particular concepts he or she only believes because of hard evidence. Scientists talk about atoms we cannot see, planets we cannot reach, and origins we cannot prove. These "edges" of the scientific frontier become matters of faith, though hardly ever recognized as such. The challenge of the evangelical task of witnessing to people who want everything proven is to find that middle ground where faith and facts can converse intelligently.

The term *seeing* has greater meaning than merely observing with the physical sense of sight. *Seeing* also can mean *understanding*. Along with such comprehension comes security, for we no longer fear what we come to understand. Understanding is the driving need of a person who wants proof before believing. If we can get him or her to understand Christianity in terms he or she can accept, he or she may no longer be afraid to commit to belief in Jesus Christ. When that happens in the evangelical effort, truly "seeing *is* believing."

Therefore, challenged by persons who demand proof, we prepare and witness the best we can. Then we pray that those to whom we witness will move into the category described so often in the New Testament, "If anyone has ears to hear, let him hear" (Mark 4:23).

Merriam-Webster's Collegiate Dictionary, 10th ed., s.v. "rationalism."

Scriptures Cited: Mark 4:23; John 20:19, 25, 28; Romans 1:20

About the Author: Dr. Everett Leadingham is the editor of the Dialog Series for the Church of the Nazarene, Kansas City, Missouri. Portions of this chapter were adapted from an unpublished manuscript by Lyle Pointer and Brint Montgomery. Used by permission; all rights reserved.

CHAPTER 9

Talking to Those Who Aren't Sure

by Everett Leadingham

WHAT DO THESE three statements have in common?
1. "I just don't know if church is for me."
2. "I don't know if God exists or not."
3. "I don't believe God exists."

All three are related to each other by a common thread —doubt. They are the typical expressions of persons we might meet in our evangelistic efforts. The first statement is liable to be made by someone who has had some experience with church, but no longer sees it as relevant. The second remark could come from the lips of an agnostic, a person who thinks we cannot know for sure about spiritual manners. The final assertion would be uttered by an atheist, someone who has concluded that the existence of God is a false idea.

In this chapter, we want to examine how people in these three groups think. We want to learn how to be effective evangelists to the formerly churched, agnostics, and atheists.

First, we will talk about common conversations we might have with a person in any of the three categories. Then, we will look at the unique challenges presented by each group. We will discuss first the atheists, then the agnostics, and finally the formerly churched.

According to some surveys, as many as 84 percent of Americans profess to believe that Jesus is the Son of God. Other surveys have shown that only about 55 percent attend church at least two Sundays a month. Obviously, all those who say they believe are not acting on their belief by attending services. So that means there is a large group of unchurched people we are likely to run into in an evangelistic effort. The other 16 percent would cover the agnostics and atheists among us. With fewer people willing to state publicly that they are atheists (perhaps 3 to 5 percent), that leaves around 11 to 13 percent for agnostics. So, our chances of talking to an agnostic are only slightly better than running into an avowed atheist. Our most likely encounters will be with those who have had some exposure to church.

Typical Discussions

Though there may be more that actually arise, at least four topics are likely to come up when we are having spiritual conversations with a former church attendee, an agnostic, or an atheist.

The most basic subject for discussion will be the existence of God. This is not an open question for a Christian, but for many others it is a stumbling block. People have many misconceptions about who God is. Some think of Him as a kindly grandfather. Others think of God as a stern, even cruel, judge. Both concepts miss the main character of God —love. Thinking of God as a doting, maybe senile old man would cause people to think of love only in sentimental terms and miss the accountability aspects of covenantal love. Seeing God as a harsh judge misses the concept of love altogether.

Because people struggle with inadequate concepts of who God really is, the topic arises all the time in spiritual conversations. A Christian will understand God one way, and the person to whom that Christian is witnessing will see Him in another. Hence, we have plenty of fodder for long discussions. Some, such as agnostics, will try to argue forever, seemingly never reaching a conclusion. Others, like atheists, will try to dismiss God completely from consideration. Yet, a conversation about salvation cannot go forward without first establishing at least the possibility of a salvation-providing God existing.

We must be prepared to explain why we have faith that God exists, if we want to be effective witnesses to agnostics and atheists. We need to be ready to help all the others bring their concept of God into a truer focus.

Another typical conversation will revolve around the Bible. Two aspects particularly interest persons in the groups we are discussing—the Bible's accuracy and its relevance. There are plenty of people willing to point out what they see as inconsistencies (they would call them "conflicts" or "errors") in Scripture. The agnostics particularly seem to enjoy pointing out discrepancies in different accounts of the same stories, especially reported numbers, etc. Atheists will often attack the Bible as being "too bloody" in its Old Testament descriptions, or dismiss all biblical accounts as merely human storytelling. Conversations about the Bible with those who have some church background will reveal more issues of current relevance. Such persons often have an inaccurate understanding of important scriptural passages or think that these have no meaning for our lives.

Prayer is bound to show up in conversations about spiritual matters. The agnostics and atheists have questions about the usefulness of prayer. Their doubts might range from prayer simply being a waste of time to it being the hopeless activity of deluded individuals. Those who have attended church in the past may have more questions about unanswered prayer, which may be at the heart of their disappointment or disillusionment with the Church.

Finally, there seems to be no end to those willing to state, "Christians are hypocrites. The Church is full of them!" Most of the time, these people have observed inconsistencies in Christians, who are merely human. Yet, they label them "hypocrites," and that keeps them at a distance from the Church.

We will discuss these topics in a little more detail later as we discuss specifics about each group, to which we now turn.

The Atheist Doesn't Believe in God

One day on an airplane, an evangelical Christian was talking to a man whom we will call James, an engineer from Europe whose work involved electronics. His research facilitated the development of new products and applications worldwide.

James's wife had a severe mental illness, yet she maintained a belief in God. James could not reconcile the two ideas. The Christian asked James, "Why have you concluded there is no God?"

James responded, "I have never needed God, and the evidence for God is scant at best." He went on to say, "I just don't think God exists."

After a few more minutes, the evangelist helped James to see that his conclusion is as much a faith statement as the person who believes in God. He had supposedly looked at the "evidence" and concluded "no God." Then he had lived his life as if that statement were true. His non-faith was faith nonetheless.

The Christian said to James, "You are a far more courageous man than I am."

James looked perplexed. "What do you mean?" he asked.

"You are banking on the fact that there is no God," the evangelist explained. "As thoughtful as you are, you must have considered the possibility that there is a God and that you might meet Him personally. This leaves you a bigger gambler than I am.

"If your idea that there is no God is wrong, you will be in big trouble when you meet Him. If my faith in God turns out to be false, nothing will happen to me."

This logic brought a slight smile to James's face, but he did not change his mind that day, so far as the witnessing Christian knew.

The encounter with James may be more typical of the atheists we might meet. Something in their life (maybe several events) have convinced them that God doesn't exist.

Most will be content to not have faith themselves, but to allow those other "poor, deluded folks" to believe if they want.

Other atheists, however, are not so mild-mannered. Some are actually hostile to religious faith, especially Christianity. Perhaps the most notorious was Madelyn Murray O'Hair. She is the one who successfully sued to get Christian prayer outlawed in public schools in 1963. She also founded an organization to spread her atheistic views and combat religious beliefs. Though O'Hair has been murdered and her organization is in disarray, we can still find any number of hostile atheists on the Internet.

This is a question to consider, but not necessarily to bring up directly in a conversation with an atheist. If God doesn't exist, why fight Him? A little digging may reveal that an atheist is not really fighting God, but is angry at how he or she has been treated by religious persons. It may be their sense of injustice and/or psychological damage that is driving their vicious attacks and mistaken belief in God's nonexistence.

The Agnostic Doesn't Know If God Exists

Dave lived across the street from us. We both had daughters about the same age. We both were working to support our families and attending college to prepare for a better future. Naturally, with so much in common, Dave and I found many occasions to talk together.

Dave was a typical agnostic, and his favorite topic of discussion was Christianity. So, Dave was always asking me about my faith. Did I believe Jesus was God's Son? Did I believe the Bible? Most important, *why* did I believe?

Dave was always open to different ideas, yet he remained skeptical the whole time I knew him. He enjoyed constantly bringing up dilemmas of faith. For instance, how could I believe that the Bible was written over thousands of years through the pens of human beings and still be the Word of God? Or why didn't I see the inconsistencies in the different accounts? How could God answer the prayers of two believers who prayed for opposite results? Or how could I overlook the bloody actions of some Christian armies down through history?

No matter how long we discussed any of those topics, Dave never came to a conclusion. He didn't want a resolution; he preferred to keep the argument stirred up. I have often wondered why, when an agnostic is not sure, he or she does not hope in the positive side of the argument rather than embracing the negative answer. Perhaps Dave felt safer with his doubt because it required less commitment than believing in Christ. Still, it seemed to me that his doubting was harder than believing.

The Unchurched Don't Trust Church

Carol is a person who asks questions typical of those who have been to church at some time in their past but no longer attend. These are persons who have usually simply drifted away from church attendance because it lacked importance in their lives, or they have become disappointed and disillusioned and left.

Carol told an evangelical Christian during a conversation, "My mother said that God doesn't answer prayer. She prayed for Grandfather to live, but he didn't. Does God answer prayer?"

The evangelist responded, "Does your mother love you?"

"Oh, yes," Carol said.

"Does she give you everything you ask for?"

"No," she smiled.

"In the same way, God does not give us everything we ask for. Even Jesus preferred not to die on the Cross, but God did not withdraw that circumstance from Him. The apostle Paul three times asked for healing, but God did not grant his request. Instead, God gave Paul the courage to withstand the pain of his discomfort.

"Therefore, we cannot conclude simply because God does not answer prayer that He does not love us. If God did everything we asked, wouldn't He really become simply a magic genie in the sky?"

Carol's next questions were similar to what agnostics and atheists ask. "Who wrote the Bible? What's it about? And which is true—what the Bible says or evolution?"

Taking a copy of the Bible from an end table, the Christian opened it and showed her the table of contents. She explained how God had spoken through men down through the centuries. While these men lived in different periods of history, they faithfully revealed to us that we can be right with God. The purpose of the Bible was to direct us to God and not to be a book of science. God explains in it how we, as sinning human beings, can find forgiveness.

The Bible shows us the way to salvation, even if it doesn't measure up to modern human standards of accuracy. It is the story of salvation history—how God created and then redeemed humanity from sin. Its message is meant for everyone, as these scriptures show. "For God so loved the world that he gave his only Son, so that *everyone* who believes in him will not perish but have eternal life" (John 3:16, NLT, emphasis added). "Let *everyone* who is thirsty come. Let *anyone who wishes* take the water of life as a gift" (Revelation 22:17b, NRSV, emphasis added).

After this exchange, which made sense to Carol, she asked yet another question. "Why are there so many hypocrites in the Church?" Her inquiry is based on a typical misunderstanding of what hypocrisy is.

When someone fails to behave as we think they should, we often consider that hypocrisy. Yet, hypocrisy is not the same as simple failure. Hypocrisy involves intentional deceit. Hypocrites are persons who, on purpose, try to make people think they are something other than what they really are. Hypocrites are those who put on masks or façades in order to conceal how they really are inside.

On the other hand, what is often mistaken for hypocrisy is simply failure to live up to what we had hoped. For example, we may very well promise more than we can deliver, like when we say "I'll always be there for you." When we find we are not able to "be there" at the depth someone needs, that does not make us a phony; it means we cannot perform at the level we wanted.

Sometimes, non-Christians accuse Christians of hypocrisy (that is, intentional deceit) when what they are actually seeing are the human shortcomings of Christians. Non-Christians often place higher expectations on Christians than they do anyone else. In fact, they erroneously expect Christians to be perfect. No human being is perfect in the sense that he or she can never make a mistake. Christians remain imperfect in that human sense as long as they are alive.

As a final point, the Christian witness pointed out the example of Jesus to Carol. Jesus continued to attend the synagogue and Temple despite the existence of hypocrites. Fifteen times in the Gospels the word "hypocrites" is on Jesus' lips. However, Mark 1:21 was typical of Jesus' behavior. "Jesus and his companions went to the town of Capernaum, and every Sabbath day he went into the synagogue" (NLT). Jesus never abandoned attendance no matter how difficult the others in the synagogue or Temple became for Him.

No Magic Bullet

When we are engaged in an evangelistic effort with atheists, agnostics, or those who used to attend church, we sometimes wish we had one powerful argument that would settle all their questions permanently. There is no such "magic bullet."

Constant arguing will not get us anywhere either. In fact, atheists and agnostics are probably better at it than we are, for arguing is what keeps them in the middle of their doubts. They have had lots of practice.

Instead of arguing, we need to understand their positions the best we can and answer as the Spirit leads. We must be willing to discuss, but it is important that we show love through every discussion. We need to continue to love, no matter how the conversations go. And we must keep them in our prayers.

For those who would still see the evangelistic effort with atheists, agnostics, and those disappointed with the Church as winning an argument, remember: "Everyone will know that the Lord does not need weapons to rescue his people. It is his battle, not ours" (1 Samuel 17:47a, NLT). If we rely on Him, rather than our own powers of persuasion, some will hear and accept the Good News—perhaps more than we can even imagine!

Scriptures Cited: 1 Samuel 17:47a; Mark 1:21; John 3:16; Revelation 22:17b

About the Author: Dr. Everett Leadingham is the editor of the Dialog Series for the Church of the Nazarene, Kansas City, Missouri. Portions of this chapter were adapted from an unpublished manuscript by Lyle Pointer and Brint Montgomery. Used by permission; all rights reserved.

CHAPTER 10

Different Beliefs About the Same Jesus

by Carl Leth

I WAS STANDING at the back of the sanctuary, greeting people at one of the exits after a Sunday morning service. One of our visitors approached me, returned a hearty handshake, and said, "Good morning, Father. I really enjoyed the Mass today."

He expressed a message that, in a variety of forms, is becoming more and more common in our church. I don't preach in a robe, and our worship service is probably very similar to most evangelical churches. The response of this visitor and those like him reflects a change in our ministry audience, not our worship.

The ranks of our church and our circles of ministry are increasingly populated by people from other Christian traditions. With the exception of new attenders from our own tradition, our most numerous newcomers are from the Roman Catholic Church. They are joined by people from a variety of mainline (non-evangelical) churches. Our women's Bible studies draw heavily from the community, involving a wide range of church traditions. We host an interdenominational men's Bible study that also involves many men from outside evangelical circles. We are discovering a growing group of people present among us who have come from very different church backgrounds, experiences, and understanding of what it means to be a Christian.

As a result, the conversations within our church are changing. We are being asked new questions, confronted by new perspectives. A nominal attender recently asked if I did prayers against curses as a pastoral service. The expectation was for a specialized priestly liturgy. This is just an example of our changing ministry context.

Greater openness to change and spiritual hunger are opening new doors of opportunity for ministry. This ministry is often to people who understand themselves as Christians but whose experience and understanding of their faith may be very different from ours. Our effectiveness in ministry to this growing constituency will depend on our ability to be an effective and redemptive part of this developing conversation between traditions.

Understanding the Differences

Those coming into fellowship with us come from such varied backgrounds and experience that it is impossible to identify and explain all the differences we may encounter. There are, however, some basics that will help us.

Particularly characteristic of the evangelical understanding of the Christian faith is an emphasis on decisive personal conversion. While Christian traditions generally will affirm conversion in some sense, evangelical Christians emphasize a personal encounter with Christ. Like Saul on the road to Damascus, we have been confronted by Christ, calling us to repent (turn around, completely change direction) and follow Him. John described this experience as being "born again" (3:3). It is often dramatic and always radically transforming. It changes us at our deepest personal levels and in the most practical and common issues of daily living. We understand ourselves in a new way, and we live our lives in a new way.

The New Testament describes this in terms of the kingdom of God. We have become citizens of a different Kingdom, God's kingdom brought to us in Christ. We live as strangers in this world, deeply committed to the lordship and rule of Jesus Christ.

While this is not essentially an emotional experience, we

are often deeply and profoundly affected emotionally by this new reality. Our commitment to Christ typically reflects a passion and intensity that others may find unusual and even uncomfortable. Still, we have experienced the gospel, "the power of God for the salvation of everyone who believes" (Romans 1:16), transforming our lives.

In addition to our emphasis on conversion, there are some other distinctive characteristics that nonevangelicals may find different or surprising. For example, we emphasize the authority of Scripture. We believe that it is true and is vitally relevant to every part of life. We grant the Bible an operating authority in every aspect of our lives. Perhaps we could express it this way: Rather than understanding the Bible as a book about religion, we understand the Bible to be the book about life. This results in an active, even studious, interest in reading and learning the Bible. Our persistent habit of looking to the Bible for directions for living sometimes seems strange to those who see it as a book about religion, primarily (or only) relevant to what happens in church.

Our understanding of what happens in church may also be different from what some of our new friends expect. While we emphasize the importance of corporate worship, we don't understand that simply being in church does something spiritual in us or for us. While we place a high value on effective spiritual leadership, we do not understand that the pastor does something for us or that he or she functions as an intermediary between God and us. Pastors and corporate worship are means that God uses to work in our lives and our community—as we cooperate with that grace. They don't do the work for us.

One last nontheological characteristic deserves mentioning. These newcomers will often mention the warmth of our services and the energy and passion we bring to our worship and Christian life. Our intensity of commitment and our emotional engagement are often strange, and sometimes unsettling, to outsiders. It may appear as religious excess or fanaticism, but it will also often be appealing to them.

It is important to help them understand that these expressions are not simply displays of human enthusiasm but are the overflow of lives that have been transformed. We have been forgiven, healed, made whole, and given confident hope in Christ. We cannot help but be powerfully gripped by these indescribable gifts and the abundant experience of life that we have found in Jesus.

Construction or Demolition

As in most things, it is important to begin our conversations in the right place. A key question to resolve concerns the focus of any spiritual conversation. Are we doing construction or demolition? Often our first impulse is to persuade these "outsiders" of the error of their prior church experience. Having (hopefully) thought through our own reasons for belief, we are anxious to share our conclusions about why our understanding of the faith is more biblically faithful or spiritually sound. While those conclusions may be valid, they are usually not the place to begin our conversation with these new dialogue partners.

Many of these people are not coming because they have rejected their heritage or background. They may assume a continuity with their prior experience. That is, they may not intend to reject past church experience or teaching at all. In their understanding, the evangelical pastor may be simply a different kind of priest; our worship, a different form of the Mass. They did not come meaning to reject the Pope or abandon their church history. They may simply be exploring the wider Christian community, looking for a richer experience of faith or better family ministries. They may not have an evangelical understanding of a personal relationship with Christ, but they understand themselves to be real Christians.

When I was in college, I was involved in intercollegiate debate. We would alternatively argue from either a positive or negative position on the question at issue. In our spiritual conversations, we, too, must decide whether to come from a positive or negative perspective. We need to keep our goal in mind in answering that question. We want to ultimately lead these precious brothers and sisters into a deeper, life-transforming relationship with Jesus Christ, not persuade them to reject their prior experience and teaching.

One perspective is about demolition; the other is about construction. We want to be about the construction business. We don't need to de-Christianize our conversation partners. It may be true that as we explore a deeper understanding of life in Christ, people may begin to see some of their prior understanding in a new light. We can let the Holy Spirit handle that side of the equation. Let's lift up the good news about what Kingdom life in Christ can be. Let's point higher. When we have the opportunity to "argue" our case in the affirmative or the negative, let's choose the positive.

Let me add one final word. Avoid negative criticism of others' background and experience, even when they are critical themselves. We can affirm our experience of the faith without joining their criticism. We can be sympathetic without being negative. We stand outside of those traditions. When they criticize their experience, they do it as a product of their own tradition, as a member of that family. We are outsiders. Our criticism may not be received well, or they may be troubled by it later. I make it a matter of policy never to be critical of other churches or traditions. Even when I need to teach the differences between our understanding and other traditions, I am careful to be factual, generous in spirit, and noncritical. I have never had cause to regret it.

Holy Humility

As we interact with people from other traditions, it may be our spirit, not our words, that will be our most effective resource. In every conversation, we need to bring a spirit of holy humility. That is, we need to come focused on being sure that our spirit and attitude are gracious and Christ-honoring. These may be more important, and more persuasive, than our logical reasoning.

It will help us to remember that we don't have all the answers either. We want to be learners too. Different traditions tend to reflect insight or emphasis on different aspects of the Christian faith. We may not share the conclusions of other traditions, but there are often positive lessons to learn from them that will enrich our own understanding of the faith. A gracious, humble spirit will certainly create a more open, positive atmosphere for constructive dialogue.

It may be the demonstration of our theology in our lives that presents the rich possibilities of the Christian faith most effectively. Arguments will usually be less welcome and less persuasive than example. I once had a parishioner who cursed one of my staff pastors in the foyer because he was upset that we were not, in his view, effectively evangelistic. It could be that he was correct, but the witness of his spirit didn't reflect anything our visitors would find appealing. We can be theologically or biblically correct and still get it all wrong. When we reflect and express the Spirit of Christ, we will almost certainly be tools God can use.

Building Blocks

In our conversations with these newcomers, we don't have to be negative or critical to invite them into a richer experience of Christian life. We can affirm the characteristics of Christianity that are so meaningful to us. Let's consider some positive building blocks for abundant life in Christ.

Real life. We believe that the Christian life is meant to be engagement in real life. It is not simply a religious exercise or mental assent to certain propositions about God. It is about the call to living the life of the Kingdom. It is an invitation to a radically new way of living.

Christ calls us to live His life at home, at school, in the marketplace, in the office. He changes and directs our use of time and money, our relationships and entertainment. The call to follow Christ shapes every part of how we live and who we are. It is a blueprint for living.

Christianity is not about rules and negative prohibitions. It is about learning a way of living that is rich and abundant—the life of the Kingdom. When we limit Christianity to a formal practice of religion or a moral code, we impoverish the rich life that Christ came to share with us. Christianity is living real life.

Scripture. We believe that the Bible is God's communication to us about that new way of living. It is not meant to be an obscure or mysterious religious document that is essentially limited in its use to religious professionals. It is a practical handbook for living.

To be sure, there are challenging messages and revelation of spiritual mysteries in the Bible. Bible scholars who are specialists help us understand the Bible better and more accurately. Still, for the most part, Scripture is accessible and helpful to all of us.

Scripture helps us to know what things are most important. It alerts us to dangers of wrong thinking or living. It clarifies our thinking about moral values and character. Because this is true, we work to read and understand the Bible. We try to apply the lessons it teaches us. We actively and persistently try to live our lives according to the guidance of God's Word.

Access to God. We believe that, because of Christ, we enjoy direct access to God. The writer of Hebrews expresses it this way: "We do not have a high priest who is unable to sympathize with our weaknesses, but we have one who has been tempted in every way, just as we are—yet was without sin. Let us then approach the throne of grace with confidence, so that we may receive mercy and find grace to help us in our time of need" (4:15-16). We do not require intermediaries or vicarious intercessors to plead our case or present our cause. We are invited to enjoy a personal relationship with Christ, who is our Savior, Friend, and Brother.

God is a God of relationships. He desires the opportunity to enjoy a relationship with us. We know that Jesus was born so that we might know God and come into relationship with Him. This extraordinary reality is God's plan for us.

We can live in daily relationship with Him, sharing our deepest needs, inviting Him into our most challenging problems and greatest joys. We appreciate the role of spiritual helpers and value the guidance of pastors, but these spiritual leaders serve to facilitate our personal relationship with Christ rather than serve in place of it.

For some of those who come into fellowship with us, these concepts will not be anything new. For others, these will be revolutionary ideas that suggest a radically new way of living as a Christian. As they come to understand and observe in us what Christian life can be like, they will be drawn toward Christ and into a deeper relationship with Him.

Bridges Jesus Can Use

We want to be faithful and effective partners with Christ. We can do that by helping to build positive, constructive bridges of understanding and growth to people who come from different Christian backgrounds. Sometimes the lessons they learn from us will be lessons they take back to enrich the church and community from which they come. Sometimes they will become a part of our church communities. Nevertheless, as long as we lift up Christ and point the way to a deeper relationship with Him, we can be assured that, wherever they choose to worship, they will be closer to the One they worship.

We have good news. Jesus Christ has broken into our lives in a personal way. He shapes, directs, and enables our living day by day. He is intimately involved in our lives and concerned about everything that affects us. In Him, we have discovered life, abundant life. It is a gift that is available to all of God's children. Let's celebrate it, embody it, and point to it.

There may be someone around us who is waiting to discover what God has shared with us. So, when someone greets me at the door with "Good morning, Father. I enjoyed the Mass," I just say a heartfelt welcome and a thank you. And I pray that God will help us to be a means of grace to this new brother or sister.

Scriptures Cited: John 3:3; Romans 1:16; Hebrews 4:15-16

About the Author: Dr. Carl Leth is senior pastor of First Church of the Nazarene, Detroit, Michigan.

Cults: The Misguided Believers

PEOPLE WHO BELONG to cults are, for the most part, people just like you and me. They may be our neighbors, friends, or even relatives. Most are white and middle-class, with a year or two of college and a desire to find happiness and self-fulfillment. Most have nominal religious backgrounds. As children they were exposed to some Sunday School or church experience, but they didn't come from deeply religious families.

Why are these normal people drawn into what are sometimes pretty bizarre cults?

Theology is not the drawing card. You don't have to be a psychiatrist or a theologian to conclude that cults are meeting needs. People would not be flocking to gurus, self-improvement groups, and pseudo Christian cults if something weren't happening. Some Christians think people join cults primarily for religious or theological reasons. That's not true.

The story of a young man named John illustrates this. He was dating a girl who had gotten involved with a cultic group through a friend of hers. She invited John to join too.

"She kept bugging me to join," John said. "But I'm a skeptic and don't do things unless I want to. One day her birthday was approaching and she said to me, 'Well, you know what you can get me for my birthday?'

"'No, what?' I answered.

"'Come to the meeting.' So I went to the meeting, and everyone was so incredibly nice to me that it made me think.

It was unbelievable. I never had known people who were so nice to me. I liked what I saw. About a week later I went back, and the week after that I went back again, and I kept going."

It can be as simple as that.

People are recruited in three basic ways: (1) by a friend or relative who is already a member of the cult, (2) by someone unknown to the recruit who befriends or persuades him or her, or (3) through a cult-sponsored activity, such as a seminar, Bible study, lecture, or free consultation.

Cults often promise more than they can deliver. They not only offer solutions to spiritual dilemmas, but they often hold out the promise of increased communication skills, healing of mind and body, personal happiness and prosperity, and even the resolution of international political conflict.

Besides offering such positive outcomes, cults have several characteristics in common. Usually, *the leadership is centered in a strong person,* who may be the founder. This person controls all aspects of the group. The cult believes that it is the recipient of a unique revelation of either a *new truth* or a *new interpretation of Scripture.* And it is not unusual for these groups to have *other authoritative writings* in addition to the Bible. From their new truth and extrabiblical sources spring *different understandings of Jesus* than those held by orthodox Christians. Most of the time, cults *reject the rest of Christianity,* believing that all other churches are wrong and only they are right.

Who Are the Targets?

Wounded people are vulnerable. The recruitment strategy of any cult can include targeting people who are experiencing problems in their lives. Cults look for people who are feeling depressed, lonely, unloved.

One young woman had a troubled background, which included child abuse. She struggled with what she felt were demonic powers in her life. Then she met a small band of people who seemed able to help her.

"When I got to this place," she said, "everybody was so

happy, and all the people were so full of love. I had never seen anything like that."

The people accepted her just as she was.

"When I got into that environment of total love and acceptance, it just sucked me in."

Stressed out people are vulnerable. Many people who get involved with cults report that when they were recruited, they were experiencing stress. Usually, they were undergoing some kind of personal transition: between high school and college, between jobs, between marriages.

People are also vulnerable when they are facing financial pressures, academic problems, the loss of a loved one, or a move to a new city. Young adults often cite communication problems with parents or the break-up with a boyfriend or girlfriend.

The Substitute Family

Cults not only direct their energy to the spiritual concerns of their members, they also address a whole range of human problems. And one way many cults attempt to solve some of the common problems of life—problems like a lack of encouragement and money—is to become a kind of substitute family for the people.

Religious cults, especially those structured as communes, often operate in an environment sealed off from the rest of the world. The "family" provides food, shelter, and all the necessities of life. In fact, the cult frequently provides jobs for the members and sometimes arranges marriages. People who have what psychologists call "dependency needs" are attracted to this kind of security available in cults.

An important drawing card for many cult recruits is the charismatic, authoritarian personality of the leader. The newer cults often have living leaders who inspire, comfort, and provide a sense of direction for the converts. Cult leaders not only give spiritual guidance and convince followers that their version of the "truth" is unique, they also create and enforce the everyday rules of the community.

Yet, the converts don't see these people as controlling, manipulative, deceivers. The members see their leaders as strong, idealistic, caring pathfinders who can dispel confusion and uncertainty about all areas of life. A god in the flesh is easier for some people to believe in.

In those cults where the founder is no longer alive, his or her influence is reinforced by continual reference to past exploits and through the sacred writings of the deceased person.

Though people are not primarily attracted to cults because of the cult's theology, converts are soon indoctrinated. So Christians who want to win these people for Christ must recognize those who join cultic movements are convinced of the truth their group teaches. Cult members need information to help them identify the false teaching they have adopted. This calls for caring, patient, informed witness on the part of Christians.

To help us in this task, let's examine more closely two examples of misguided believers we are likely to know personally: Mormons and Jehovah's Witnesses.

The Church of Jesus Christ of Latter-Day Saints

The members of the church founded by Joseph Smith in 1830 are commonly known as Mormons or LDS. They part company with Christianity in several of their beliefs.

Mormonism teaches God is married and was once a man. Humans are literally the children of God. As the same species, we each have the potential to become a god. The Mormons have three extra volumes of "holy" scripture besides the Bible. They consider these newer scriptures more reliable.

One of the problems Christians have in witnessing to LDS people and in learning what they believe is that both groups use many of the same religious words, but the meaning is very different. The Mormon church has redefined most words Christians use to explain their faith.

When a Christian speaks of being saved or of the assurance of heaven, a Mormon will readily agree. Yet, the average Christian doesn't realize that to the Mormon, "saved by grace" means everyone will be resurrected through Christ. Mormons believe the resurrected masses will be placed in different levels of heaven. The more good works the person has done, the higher in heaven they get to go.

All those who reach heaven will live forever. And, in the Mormon view, most people—even non-Mormons—will reach heaven. Still, not everyone will have what Mormons refer to as "eternal life." To the Mormon, eternal life is more than immortality. It is the ability to eternally procreate and give life. So, contrary to John 3:36 and Luke 20:35, Mormons say eternal life is the ability to live forever in the family unit. This means producing millions of spirit children to inhabit the earth they will form. Only those who are faithful Mormons, married in a Mormon temple, will be granted this "eternal life."

What attracts people to the Mormon church are its family-oriented programs, its positive view of human nature, and its teaching that almost everyone will be saved and will live in some level of heaven.

Mormonism also appeals to people confused by the many different religions and disturbed that all Christians do not belong to the same denomination. Such people relate to Joseph Smith's search for the only true church.

As God gives us opportunity to share our faith in Christ with our Mormon friends, we need to remember that years of false teaching are not usually reversed in one conversation. Most Mormons who come to Christ have at least one Christian friend witnessing to them for months or years. We Christians also need to be sensitive to the emotional trauma Mormons go through when they leave that faith for a new life in Christ.

Jehovah's Witnesses

Though Christians today know the Jehovah's Witnesses primarily because of their stand on blood transfusions and aggressive door-to-door evangelism, the organization grew from the seeds of adventist teaching.

Prophecy about end times was on the mind of Charles Taze Russell when he founded the organization in 1884 in Pennsylvania. He called it Zion's Watch Tower and Tract Society. This was named after the magazine he had started five years earlier, *Zion's Watch Tower.* Russell believed, as adventists taught, that Christ had invisibly returned to the Earth in 1874. Russell also began predicting the world would end in 1914.

Russell died in 1916. A few months after Russell's death, Joseph F. Rutherford took over the society. Rutherford made changes. He set 1925 as the new date for the world's end, as we know it. Rutherford solidified Russell's membership gains, then weathered mass desertions from the society after his 1925 prophecy failed. In 1931, he began calling society members Jehovah's Witnesses. Then he launched the society's door-to-door work. He began teaching Christ had returned in 1914.

Rutherford died in 1942 and was replaced by Nathan H. Knorr. Knorr inherited 65,000 "publishers," or Witnesses who promoted the society's message. When he died in 1977, there were 2.25 million Jehovah's Witnesses.

During Knorr's tenure, the society produced its own translation of the Bible, completed in 1961 and called the *New World Translation of the Holy Scriptures.* The translation distorts Christian doctrine to suit the society's beliefs.

One of the five men who translated the Witnesses' Bible was Frederick W. Franz. He was a vice president under Knorr, and succeeded him in 1977. Franz helped shape current beliefs. In 1966, he wrote a book that implied the world would end in 1975. Jehovah's Witnesses took the book so seriously that some began selling their homes and property. In 1974, the society praised members who sold their homes and devoted themselves to full-time Jehovah's Witnesses service.

Again, the end failed to arrive, and society membership dropped sharply. Rumblings and discontent resulted in nearly 30,000 "apostates" being expelled in 1978. In spite of all the problems, the society has endured because of its preoccupation with end times. The theme remains a dominant part of their magazines and books.

Author Edmund C. Gruss chose to name his book on Jehovah's Witnesses history and beliefs, *Apostles of Denial.* That was a good choice because Jehovah's Witnesses deny most of the key doctrines of the Christian faith. They deny the Trinity, the deity of Jesus Christ, the person of the Holy Spirit, the bodily resurrection of Christ, His visible second coming, humanity's eternal soul, the existence of hell, and a heavenly home for all believers.

Jehovah's Witnesses refuse to observe religious and secular holidays. They believe Christmas and Easter celebrations grew out of pagan practices. They consider birthdays, Mother's Day, and Father's Day as creature worship—a kind of idol worship. Even national holidays are off-limits, because they encourage loyalty to a government instead of loyalty to Jehovah. This ban on holidays serves one more purpose. It isolates Jehovah's Witnesses from society. Isolation is a practice common to many cults.

Witnessing to Cult Members

Jesus died to save Mormons and Jehovah's Witnesses as much as He died for anyone else. Christians need to tell them that. Here are a few suggestions about how to witness to persons in cults.

Witness with love. Love must be the primary motive for our witnessing. Our motive should not be to prove we are right and they are wrong. Winning an argument is not enough. We need a compassion that realizes that persons are involved in cults because they want God's favor. These are people who need to hear about God's grace, freely given.

Contrast the cult's message and the Christian gospel. Listen to what the cult member believes. Then tell him or her that the gospel message is one of hope. The good news is about the salvation we can experience, because of the death, burial, and resurrection of Jesus Christ.

Outline the gospel preached by the apostles (1 Corinthians 1:23; 15:1-4; Colossians 1:22-23; 2 Timothy 2:8; 1 Peter 1:3). Explain that the penalty for preaching a gospel different from the apostles' is eternal condemnation (Galatians 1:8-9).

Look at the context of scriptures they use. Be alert for misinterpretation and hop-scotching through the Bible. Call their attention to the setting of the passages, when they are quoting isolated verses out of context. To do this, read the verses before and after the cited verse, in a generally accepted version of the Bible (such as the King James Version or New International Version).

Describe your new life in Christ. Tell the person how you became a Christian and what it is like to be one. Use scripture. Stress that the Bible says a person can be saved only by accepting Christ as Lord and Savior.

Give the cult member orthodox Christian literature. After your talk, give the person some materials that explain the gospel message. Some organizations provide tracts specifically for members of certain cults, and are happy to make them available. Invite the person to read the literature and check the Bible references.

A Final Word

Remember that people who belong to cults are, for the most part, people just like you and me. Do not be afraid of the opportunities to spend time with such persons. Look on those times as God-given.

Build a relationship with the person, as much as you can. Witness to him or her about God's love as often as you can. Be sure to tell the person that you will be praying for him or her —and then do it.

Scriptures cited: Luke 20:35; John 3:36; 1 Corinthians 1:23; 15:1-4; Galatians 1:8-9; Colossians 1:22-23; 2 Timothy 2:8; 1 Peter 1:3

This chapter has been adapted from material that originally appeared in *Misguiding Lights?* Stephen M. Miller, editor (Kansas City: Beacon Hill Press of Kansas City, 1991).

CHAPTER 12

The West Meets the East

Since the 1960s, many North Americans and Europeans have been interested in religions practiced for centuries in the Orient. Two of the most prominent of these traditional religions are Buddhism and Hinduism. In recent years, many people have immigrated to North America from countries where Buddhism or Hinduism is the dominant religion.

It is very likely that Christians will run into someone who is either a Buddhist or Hindu in everyday life. Many of them own the businesses that provide the services we need. Others are the disillusioned ones who have converted. If we are to witness to them about Christianity, we must know something about their religion.

In this chapter we will first look at the beliefs held by Buddhists, then examine the Hindu religion. Finally, as an example of how we can witness to persons who practice these religions, we will look at how one American Buddhist was converted to Christianity.

Who Is Buddha?

If you were to ask that question to a few of the 320 million people on earth today who call themselves Buddhists, some would say he is like a rabbit's foot. "He brings me good fortune." Others would say he was the wisest man who ever lived. Still others consider him the lord of the universe, though most Buddhists do not consider him a god.

Buddha was born in a rural rice farming area that his father ruled in Northern India. Legend says his father learned from a local fortune-teller that Buddha was going to become a wise man one day, and that he would probably leave home. This meant Buddha's father would have no one to take over his kingdom after he died. So Buddha's father decided if he could surround his son with the best that money could buy, his son might stay.

Buddha, born with the name Siddhartha Gautama (si DAHR tah GOU tah mah), was also protected from as many of the unpleasant realities of life as possible. For example, when he traveled throughout the countryside, his father ordered that all the sick and elderly should stay inside. The father didn't want his son to see these people working hard in the rice paddies.

Then one day, without warning, the young Buddha slipped out of the estate for an eye-opening tour of the kingdom. He saw things he had never seen before. He asked a servant traveling with him what was wrong with the people.

The servant pointed each person out and replied, "That person is old; the other is diseased. That man is wise, and the other is dead."

The prince became upset at all the suffering he saw as he continued to tour his father's kingdom. So he decided to do something about it. He was going to do what many other young Indian men had done: renounce all possessions and become a monk. He would live a life of self-denial. That meant leaving his home, his family, even his wife and baby son.

So he left his comfortable surroundings and his inheritance to begin training under the best teachers of his day. Like other monks, or ascetics, of his day, he probably lay on beds of nails, walked on hot coals, and starved himself in extended fasts. All this in a search for answers to the questions that plagued him.

After six years of this, he decided he was wasting his time. So he found himself a big Bo tree, sat down, and resolved not to get up until he had solved the riddles of this life. After 49 days and nights of meditation, the story goes, he reached what Buddhists call enlightenment. He finally had all the answers to life's suffering. That was how he got the name Buddha, which means "the Enlightened One."

What Buddhists Believe

As there are many denominations in Christianity, there are many sects in Buddhism. The more orthodox Buddhism, especially popular in Southeast Asia, is the Buddhism of the elders. It's also know as Theravada (ther ah VAH dah) or Hinayana (hie nah YAH nah). These Buddhists believe that by renouncing the world and all its pleasures, and by meditation and right living, they can eliminate suffering and attain the highest goal of Buddhism, nirvana.

Nirvana is as close as these Buddhists get to the Christian idea of heaven. Nirvana, where they believe Buddha went after he died, has been described as the transformation of a person's identity and awareness. However, it's more like the extinction of self as the person merges with the universe.

Because Buddhists in this sect believe selfishness is the cause of the world's problems, they practice self-denial as they journey toward enlightenment and nirvana. The monks follow about 250 commandments and the nuns 500. Women have more rules to follow, because being a woman is considered inferior to being a man. A woman, for example, must be reborn as a male before she can progress on to nirvana. Women, in other words, are women because of bad karma. "Karma" is the Buddhist teaching that says we reap what we sow, if not in this life perhaps in the next or the next.

The goal of each person, then, is that over a period of many lifetimes he (not she) will eventually achieve that level of enlightenment Buddha reached as he sat under the tree. Only then will the cycle of reincarnation and suffering end.

A second branch of Buddhism is called Mahayana (mah hah YAH nah). It is popular in Vietnam, Hong Kong, Taiwan, China, Korea, Japan, and in countries to which these people have immigrated, like the United States. Mahayana Buddhism broke off from Theravada Buddhism in the first two centuries after Christ. Some scholars speculate Christians caused the break, since Mahayana Buddhism seems to merge Buddhist philosophy with some Christian doctrine. For example, some sects springing from Mahayana Buddhism worship Buddha as a god. Yet, Buddha never claimed to be a god, or even a messenger sent from God. In fact, on the subject of God, Buddha was very quiet. The Amida (ah MEE dah) sect of Buddhism also appears to merge Buddhism with Christianity. These Buddhists believe in heaven and in the doctrine of grace that can set you free from the "wheel of suffering."

Yet, Buddhism, from its very beginning, was never based on a system of grace. Hope for the Buddhist came not through some gift by a compassionate god. It came through a system of works, known as the Eightfold Path. This path to enlightenment requires Buddhists to pursue right knowledge, attitude, speech, action, living (occupation), effort, mindfulness (meditation), and composure. The first two deal with wisdom, the next three with conduct, and the last three with mental discipline.

Another form of Buddhism is called Nichiren Shoshu (NE-sure-an SHOW-shu), also known as NSA (Nichiren Shoshu Academy). A radical Japanese Buddhist monk called Nichiren founded it in the 13th century A.D. Today over 20 million people follow his religion in 115 countries around the world.

Buddhists from other denominations think of it as materialistic Buddhism. That's because NSA members often chant for things like jobs and new girlfriends. What they chant is a phrase that Nichiren said was the essence of *Lotus Sutra,* a book containing what Buddhists believe are the highest teachings of Buddha. The four-word phrase chanted is, literally translated, "Devotion, mystic law of life and death, cause and effect, and sound or vibration." Buddhists say that by kneeling and chanting this phrase, they get into the rhythm of the universe, and good things begin to happen.

The chanting is directed toward a piece of paper. On this paper, written in Chinese, Japanese, and Sanskrit, are the names of Shinto, Hindu, and Buddhist gods, called "forces of the universe." Also on the paper is the name of the sect's founder, Nichiren.

Some people laugh at the idea of worshiping a piece of paper, but a lot of people worship paper. It's called money.

Hindu Teachings

Hinduism is an old and exotic religion. It contains all the bizarre trappings of dark and mysterious Asia. Nearly naked holy men meditating on mountainsides. Long-haired, bearded gurus wrapped in gold and scarlet robes. Head-shorn monks dressing stone idols. It is an ancient philosophy of reincarnation, cosmic consciousness, repetitious chanting, and sweet incense.

Two concepts lie at the core of Hindu teachings.

Impersonal God-force. Hindu philosophers often speak of "The Absolute," a sort of universal spirit called "Brahman." Hindus believe that the world is really "Brahman in disguise." In other words, all matter, and especially biological and human life, are only temporary manifestations or "vibrations" coming from this universal spirit.

As a result, for many Hindus there is no difference between the creator and the creation. All things, including people, are essentially "God," even if we are unaware of this. This idea is called *pantheism,* a word that comes from the Greek *pan,* meaning "all," and *theos,* meaning "God." The word *pantheism* means "all is God."

This idea is quite at odds with the Christian teaching about God. The God of Scripture is an infinite, all-powerful, loving personal Creator who is distinct from and above His creation.

Reincarnation. The second basic teaching of Hinduism is reincarnation. This idea of rebirth into a new body has become popular and trendy in the last few decades, especially in influential circles, such as Hollywood. One reason some people are eager to accept reincarnation is it gives them an excuse for putting off moral choices. After all, we'll get another chance in the next life.

There is much speculation about the details of reincarnation, but at its core, the doctrine simply says all forms of life are somehow reborn after death. In the case of humans, this means we are reborn into a better status if we have behaved well. On the other hand, if we have lived a bad life, we can be reborn as a person who pays for his or her previous sins by experiencing suffering and poverty. Like the Buddhists, the Hindus call these past sins "karma."

Reincarnation does not mesh with the central Christian teaching of resurrection. Christians believe that each believer rises after death to an eternal life in heaven.

Living the Hindu Religion

Religious practice takes many forms in Hinduism. These forms are often colorful and bizarre. The holy city of Rishikesh in north India sits beside the Ganges River, nestled among the foothills of the Himalaya Mountains. If you walk a mile upstream from the town, you can see the strange and varied faces of Hinduism. Naked holy men, known as ascetics, paint their bodies with bright colors and sit on rocks in the middle of the river. They will meditate for hours, sometimes for days.

Monasteries line the river bank. These sacred houses are filled with novice disciples who wander about with orange robes and shaved heads. Enlightened spiritual teachers called "gurus" preside over the monasteries. Other gurus live in caves or huts in the hills, where they perform meditation and yoga for years, in an attempt to attain salvation.

For the Hindu, a guru is more than just a pastor or priest. The guru is a man who has supposedly attained enlightenment after thousands of reincarnations. Some gurus are even worshiped as divine figures, more powerful than the gods. Gurus usually demand complete obedience from their disciples. The disciples dutifully live spartan lives, enduring long hours of manual labor, meditation, and little sleep.

As you walk past small temples in the hills and along the river, you can hear chanting and chimes, and smell the sweet aroma of incense. Inside the temples there is an eerie half-light. Scores of stone and wooden idols peer down at worshipers through the smoky haze of flickering candles.

There are literally millions of gods in Hinduism, and people worship them in a simple ceremony. The devout offer the god flowers, food, incense, and prayer.

How a Buddhist Became a Christian

The story of a young man named James illustrates the popularity of eastern religions in North America today. Perhaps we can learn better how to witness to our Buddhist or Hindu friends from his conversion to Buddhism and back to Christianity.

When he was a child growing up in a small, rural town in Montana, James attended Sunday School for about two years. His parents, however, had other pressing concerns in raising their family, and attended only rarely. He can't remember discussing spiritual matters at the dinner table.

At least not until he became a Buddhist in college.

During those growing up years, he came to realize that a lot of people thought church was important. Yet, very few seemed to take their religion seriously during the rest of the week. His parents, for example, wanted their children to learn about God, but they didn't live a life that showed them how to worship the God talked about in Sunday School.

By the time he was a senior in high school, James's family had moved to California. He had a lot of questions about spiritual issues: Why was he alive? Where would he go after he died?

The only person he found in school who seemed interested in spiritual things was his locker partner, Russ. He was excited about his newfound faith in Buddhism and chanting. However, that seemed too bizarre to James.

After high school, he moved back to the state of his childhood and enrolled at the University of Montana. There, during a course in psychology, he became intrigued by eastern religions. That semester left him disoriented and homesick, so he migrated back home to California, where he enrolled in a local university. He soon found that many of his friends, even some of the very conservative ones, had gotten interested in eastern philosophy.

In one of his classes, he ran into his former locker partner, Russ. This time he was interested in what Russ had to say about his religion. Russ said, "If you want to change the problems in society, you must first change yourself." That made sense to James.

Russ explained that chanting produces vibrations that help us get in harmony with the basic components of the universe. Then he invited James to give it a try. A couple days later he gave James some magazines about Buddhism, which explained how "scientific" it all was. It seemed reasonable to James that the answers to life's tough questions would come from the Orient. After all, their civilization had been around a lot longer than ours. And Buddhism had been around long before Christianity.

Within two weeks, James was attending meetings on Buddhism. What a different experience! The chanting in these meetings sounded to him like angels singing in the heavens. There were people from many different races. And the smell of incense added to the mystery of it all. He wondered, *Could this be the answer to the problems we are facing as a planet?*

For the next 14 years, James practiced Buddhism, zealously converting over 54 people to Nichiren Shoshu. Then his faith began to sour.

In the discussions, study sessions, and business meetings he attended, he felt free to talk about whatever was on his mind. However, when he started asking questions about God and where the money was going, then James started drawing opposition.

One morning he accompanied a group of Buddhists to a meeting with leaders at the North American headquarters for NSA. There, when they questioned the staff about money, all they got was name-calling and stares. As a protest, they left the meeting *en masse.*

James was beginning to wonder how the compassionate Buddha fit into all this. Why were the NSA leaders unwilling to be open about the finances? And why did they react with similar disapproval to his questions about God? They worshiped Buddhist gods every morning, which they called "forces of the universe." Yet, James wondered why these divine forces didn't protect a young black girl in the group from being killed. Or why they didn't keep another member from hanging herself in despair.

James decided he was asking the right questions to the wrong people. He became a spiritually broken man. He felt totally lost.

God used a Christian architect friend of James's who had gently tried witnessing to him before. She came into the blueprint store where he was working, and during their conversation, he told her about his spiritual emptiness. She responded, "I've been praying for you." James was deeply moved by her concern.

The next morning, there was a package waiting for James at work. It had a card on top that read, "Ask and it will be given to you; seek and you will find; knock and the door will be opened to you" (Matthew 7:7). In the package were two books: one by J. Isamu Yamamoto called *Beyond Buddhism,* and another by Josh McDowell, *More Than a Carpenter.* After reading these books, James wondered, *Could this be the perfect Master he had been seeking?*

Soon after this, another Christian businessman learned of James's spiritual confusion and loaned him a Bible. Reading the Gospel of John, James quickly discovered that Jesus was utterly different from the Christ that Buddhist leaders taught. He'd often heard Nichiren Shoshu leaders mockingly exclaim, "Can you believe a religion that worships a dead man on a cross?"

Yet, in that amazing Book was the Living Master, the One who was not reincarnated, but resurrected, the One James had sought so desperately in human teachings.

James had found the Truth at last!

This chapter has been adapted from material that originally appeared in *Misguiding Lights?* Stephen M. Miller, editor (Kansas City: Beacon Hill Press of Kansas City, 1991).

CHAPTER 13

Islam: A Search for Hope and Grace

by Randy Cloud

I WOKE FROM a deep sleep, uncertain of the hour but sure that it could not yet be morning. My sleep had been disturbed by something out of place, something that definitely did not belong in the early morning atmosphere—the lyrical voice of a man calling out in a language I did not understand over a loudspeaker outside my open window!

It took a few seconds for my drowsy mind to remember that I was not sleeping in my own bed in mid-America. I was, instead, in a hotel room in the center of Amman, Jordan. The voice shattering the morning stillness was the Arabic call of the muezzin from the powerful speakers atop the minaret of the nearest Islamic mosque: "Arise to prayer! Arise to success! Prayer is better then sleep!"

For many of us, the Islamic religion remains distant and strange. In recent years, our worldview has expanded to include the once-faraway centers of Islam, and we have been forced to think about this religious culture. Still, our understanding is often limited and consists primarily of isolated images:

☐ unforgettable photos of United States airliners being rammed into the twin World Trade Center towers, piloted by Islamic hijackers.

☐ men adorned in long beards and long robes and red-and-white kafiyahs.*

- the shining gold roof of the Dome of the Rock in the middle of Old Jerusalem.
- prostrate figures of Muslims praying toward Mecca.
- chanting mobs, shaking their fists in political and moral outrage.
- strange-sounding and hard-to-pronounce Arabic names of people and cities.
- mosques with a crescent moon high atop their towers.

The word *Islam* brings a variety of emotions to westerners today, from a feeling of fear to a sense of anger to a certain strangeness. Islam brings to mind more images of war than religion for most of us. Our natural inclination may be to keep these people at arm's length. Yet, as we explore this religion from a Christian vantage point, we will need to keep firmly in mind that Muslims, like ourselves, are people for whom Christ died.

We, as Christians, will find more and more opportunities to share the Christian message of hope and grace with these worshipers of Allah as Islam finds growing numbers of adherents in our own communities here at home, far from places like Amman, Jordan. To be ready to seize these unique chances to witness, our understanding needs to be enhanced and our strategies rehearsed. In this chapter, we will look at Islam, the fastest-growing religion in the world. We want to be able to better engage in spiritual conversations with Muslims we will undoubtedly encounter in our neighborhoods, schools, malls, and communities.

A Short History of Islam

Let's take a brief look at the beginnings of Islam, a religion that started in the same general region of the world as Judaism and Christianity. Islam, founded by Muhammad, traces its roots to Abraham through Hagar and Ishmael as found in the stories of Genesis 16, 17, and 21.

Muhammad was born in A.D. 570 in Mecca, at that time the central city of the Arabian Peninsula. At about age 40, as he prayed in a cave one day, Muhammad heard a voice command him to recite the words supernaturally impressed upon his mind. Being illiterate, he could not write them down, so he memorized them. These words, direct from the mouth of Allah, became the Islamic Qur'an (sometimes spelled Koran), the holy scriptures of Muslims.

In his hometown of Mecca, Muhammad began to preach his doctrines. He insisted that there was only one God. The 360 deities worshiped in Mecca were false—or 359 of them were. One ancient religious strand associated with Abraham had spread throughout the area and worshiped a God called Allah. ("Allah" is simply the Arabic phrase for "one God.") Muhammad believed that their belief in this God was superior to all others. He began to preach and teach that Allah was the one true God that had encountered him in the cave.

Muhammad was resisted and persecuted in Mecca. Some of his followers were put to death. Nevertheless, soon the nearby city of Medina invited Muhammad to make his headquarters there. On July 22, 622, the devotees made their move to Medina (City of the Prophet). All Islamic calendars mark this date as their beginning. The move to Medina is called the *Hijira* (the Flight).

By the time of his sudden death just 10 years later, Muhammad, as the spiritual and civil leader, had subjected most of the Arab world to Islamic rule. Those Arabs who did not convert were driven out or killed. Within a century, Islamic armies had established a huge empire that stretched from Spain in the west to India in the east. Soon the empire reached into eastern Europe in the north and to the sub-Sahara regions of Africa in the south. They were the dominant world empire in the west for almost 600 years while Europe developed slowly through the Middle Ages. The Christian Crusades tried to dislodge the Islamic Empire from the Holy Land during this period and were largely ineffective against the superior Muslim military forces.

Over time, a number of different sects of Islam developed. The principal ones are the Sunnis, the Sufis, and the Shiites. The Sunnis appear to be the more moderate group.

The Sufis are those who have added mysticism to the rather legalistic, cold, and formal worship of mainstream Islam. From the Shiites come many of the extremists, radicals, and terrorists who push to the forefront Muhammad's sayings about *jihad* or holy war against the infidels. Jews, capitalists, and communists are the "great Satans" against which the radical Shiites war. Islamic fundamentalists wage terrorist campaigns in many parts of the world. Still, most followers of Islam are sincere, peace-loving people. They firmly believe in their religion and, like Christians, are very mission-ary-minded, but most do not believe their faith should be forced on others. They will let you know that mainstream Muslims are not like the terrorists who use Allah's name to justify their violence.

About 1 billion people on our planet claim an allegiance to the Islamic faith, second only to Christianity. The most populous Islamic nation is Indonesia, where 100 million believers declare that "There is no god but Allah, and Muhammad is his messenger." Turkey, Russia, and large sections of Africa also support large numbers of Muslim devotees.

Basics of Islamic Religion

Islam is one of the three major world religions, along with Judaism and Christianity, that profess monotheism, or the belief in a single God. In the Arabic language, the word *Islam* means "surrender" or "submission"—to the will of God. A follower of Islam is called a Muslim, which in Arabic means "one who surrenders to God." Islam's central teaching is that there is only one all-powerful, all-knowing God, and this God created the universe.

The Muslim religion is built around five essential beliefs.

Allah: Muslims believe there is one true God, Allah. He is so far above us that He is unknowable. To speak of a personal relationship with God or to call Him "Father," as Christians do, is blasphemy. Allah is sovereign, running the universe as He pleases. Everything that happens is His will. Allah is the author of both good and evil. He blesses those who obey Him and punishes those who don't. This predestined view of life leads many to shrug, "It is the will of Allah," when challenged by adversity.

The Koran sees Jesus as a prophet, but not as a Savior or the Son of God. Jesus could not be God's Son, for God has no Son. Jesus was only a messenger of Allah. According to Muslims, Jesus did not die on the Cross and was therefore never resurrected. Jesus did not bring the final revelation from God; Muhammad did that.

Some have wondered if the God of Islam is the same God of Christianity. While there are historic connections (Muhammad likely had contact with both Jews and Christians during his lifetime) there are so many key differences that most Christians do not associate Allah with the one true God they serve and worship. Key to these differences is the lack of grace and relationship found in the person of Allah.

Angels: Allah created angels from light. They do not have what humans call "free will" but obey Allah instinctively. Angels protect humans, keep Allah's records, deliver his messages, and administer his punishment. Two angels are assigned to each person. One writes down every bad deed; the other records good deeds.

Revelation: The Muslims believe that four books are inspired by Allah. The first three are the Torah (the first five books of our Bible), the Psalms of David, and the Gospel of Christ. However, they believe that Jews and Christians have allowed their sacred books to be corrupted. Therefore Allah gave one last perfect revelation from God—the Koran. For Muslims, the Koran has precedence over the Bible.

Prophets: Adam, Noah, Abraham, Moses, David, and Jesus were all prophets, but the greatest of them was Muhammad.

Judgment: Those who have obeyed Allah and Muhammad will be rewarded at the Judgment by being sent to the Muslim heaven, called "paradise." It is a place of pleasure. Others will be condemned to the torments of hell. Muslims do not know whether they are on the road to paradise or hell. They know they must earn their salvation by accumulating as many good deeds as possible and hope for the best.

Beyond these five doctrines, all Muslims faithfully observe these five practices, called the Five Pillars of Islam.

The Creed: In order to become a Muslim, one must declare publicly, "There is no god but Allah, and Muhammad is his prophet." This is to be repeated many times a day.

Prayer: At five appointed times during the day, the Muslim is to recite prescribed prayers in a prescribed position (standing, kneeling, face to the ground, facing Mecca).

Alms for the Poor: Muhammad was himself an orphan and thus had sensitivity for the poor. At the end of each year, devout Muslims are to give 2½ percent of their wealth in an offering for the poor.

Fasting: During the Islamic month of Ramadan, devout Muslims are expected to fast from sunrise to sunset. Most families eat a meal before dawn and another after dark. The fast is aimed at promoting self-control and empathy with the poor. Eating, drinking, smoking, and sexual comforts are forbidden during this time.

Pilgrimage: If physically able, Muslims are expected to make a pilgrimage (called *hajj*) to Mecca in Saudi Arabia. Many Muslims also visit Medina, where Muhammad is buried, and Jerusalem, where the famous Dome of the Rock commemorates the site where Muhammad ascended to heaven to visit Allah. Mecca, Medina, and Jerusalem are the three holy cities of Islam.

Other distinctive Muslim practices include avoiding pork, refraining from gambling, and not drinking alcoholic beverages. Males and females often have distinct dress codes as well. Women are generally accorded less status than men. Of all Muslim institutions, the mosque is the most important place for the public expression of Islamic religious and communal identity. In the United States today there are over 1,000 mosques with nearly 2 million Muslim adherents.

Christians Talking to Muslims

It may seem difficult for Christians to find common ground with Muslims. Islam and Christianity share a common thread of history back to Abraham. However, spiritual dialog is difficult to discover when Islam refutes just about every core doctrine of Christianity. Muslims deny the authority of the Bible, original sin, the existence of the Trinity, the deity of Jesus Christ, the death and resurrection of Christ, salvation by grace through faith, and the possibility of a personal relationship with Christ. They can respect each other but must stop short of embracing the other's core beliefs and must not act as if the differences are trivial. Yet, as with any person of any background, there are common spiritual needs that are universal. There are questions of the heart and soul that Islam only accentuates but does not and cannot answer.

Confrontation is not the way for Christians to witness to Muslims. This has failed miserably for 14 centuries. Muslims, like Christians, hold sincere beliefs that are reinforced by culture and a religion that is a way of life. We, as Christians, can choose to offer words of grace and hope, not shouts of condemnation. Like Jesus' discussion with the Samaritan woman at the well, we can offer our spiritually thirsty Muslim neighbors the Living Water that will quench their soul deep thirst.

Some of the Muslims we will meet have come from a long-standing background of Islam; they were raised in this faith and their family and cultural heritage is found there. Other Muslims may be recent converts who have no family history in Islam. For either type of encounter, here are some avenues for Christians to talk to their Muslim neighbors:

A true picture of God: Muslims sincerely, desperately want to please God. But Allah is remote and far removed from their world. Christians can show Muslims that the one true God they are searching for is not far but near. He is a God who came to live with us in the person of Jesus and who continues to live with us in the person of the Holy Spirit. He is our loving Father, not a harsh taskmaster. He wants to know us—and for us to know Him. The way to God is through Jesus. Muslims are not unfamiliar with Jesus, but Christians can help them see that beyond being a prophet of God, Jesus was indeed the Son of God who makes a relationship with God possible. This is perhaps the hardest aspect of Christianity for a Muslim to accept, but it is also the most liberating truth anyone trained in the Islamic faith can discover.

Assurance of salvation: Life for Muslims is based on ritual performance and accumulation of good deeds. As I stood by the Dome of the Rock in Jerusalem, I asked a Muslim attendant the purpose of an ancient pillar that stood nearby. He replied that on this pillar a large scale will be erected on the day of Judgment. Each person's good deeds will be placed on one side, bad deeds on the other. Depending on the swing of the scale, a person's eternal fate will be determined. Muslims live without assurance of salvation and must resort to hoping for the best. Christians can share the wonderful news that, in Christ, assurance of salvation and eternal life can free each person to live in peace and confident hope each and every day. Grace is a key missing element in Islam that Christians can lovingly offer.

Common moral values: There is common ground for Muslims and Christians in the realm of ethics and morality. Muslims believe in modesty of dress, forbid premarital sex, consider abortion murder, and oppose homosexuality. The Bible and the Koran both speak of treating others with kindness, looking out for the poor, caring for the elderly, living upright lives, and pleasing God with our actions. However, the power to accomplish this kind of lifestyle comes only through the power of God working directly in our lives and not by our efforts and willpower alone. Christians can share with Muslims this secret to living righteous lives, one that concentrates more on the limitless resources of God rather than our limited human resources.

Devotion to God: Muslims probably do better than many

Christians in realizing that all of life is to be dedicated to God. For Muslims, there is no separation of life into sacred and secular. Christians can affirm, and perhaps learn from, this dedication to their faith. As I traveled on a Royal Jordanian flight, I was impressed with the sincere efforts of the Muslim man seated next to me. The plane showed a map that pointed out the location of Mecca in relation to our current flight direction. At the time of afternoon prayers, as we traveled west over the Atlantic, Mecca lay directly behind us. Yet, my neighbor managed somehow to twist his entire body around in his small plane seat to conduct his prayer-time facing Mecca. I appreciated the efforts of this Muslim devotee but also longed to share with him that dedicated ritual alone leads to an empty spiritual dead end.

Present and future life: The success of Islam has been largely in areas of the world where people have felt powerless and downtrodden. Islam offers some measure of comfort in providing tangible ways to confront the agonies of this present life with the promise of life eternal. Muslims find purpose in life by adhering to the regular structures of Islamic life, hoping to please God and gain paradise. Christianity also looks ahead to our heavenly home where all will be light and love, but it also lives out the reality of God's light and love in this life. Hope for Christians is not only based on the future but is rooted firmly in the present.

A Final Word

We, as Christians, can best share the good news of Christ with our Muslim friends as we allow the very heart of God's grace and hope to be gently but visibly noticeable in our actions and words. In this way, they may want to take a closer look at the Jesus who brings peace, healing, forgiveness, and love.

*An Arab headdress consisting of a square cloth folded to form a triangle and held on by a cord.

Scriptures cited: Genesis 16; 17; 21

About the Author: Randy Cloud is the former director of Sunday School curriculum for the Church of the Nazarene. Currently, he teaches religion at MidAmerica Nazarene University in Olathe, Kansas.

For Further Reading

Eby, J. Wesley, editor. *What Christians Believe: In Beginning English.* Kansas City: Beacon Hill Press of Kansas City, 2003.

Eck, Diana L. *A New Religious America: How a "Christian Country" Has Now Become the World's Most Religiously Diverse Nation.* San Francisco: Harper, 2001.

Leadingham, Everett, editor. *I Believe: Now Tell Me Why.* Kansas City: Beacon Hill Press of Kansas City, 1994.

McCumber, W. E. *Everybody Into the Field!: The Power of Sunday School to Transform Lives Through Evangelism.* Kansas City: Beacon Hill Press of Kansas City, 1998.

Muck, Terry C. *Those Other Religions in Your Neighborhood.* Grand Rapids: Zondervan, 1992.

Nees, Thomas G. *Compassion Evangelism: Meeting Human Needs.* Kansas City: Beacon Hill Press of Kansas City, 1996.

Netland, Harold. *Encountering Religious Pluralism.* Downers Grove, Ill.: InterVarsity Press, 2001.

Pointer, Lyle and Jim Dorsey. *Evangelism in Everyday Life: Sharing and Shaping Your Faith.* Kansas City: Beacon Hill Press of Kansas City, 1998.

Swift, Donald C. *Religion and the American Experience.* New York: M. E. Sharpe, 1998.

Toler, Stan. *ABCs of Evangelism: An Easy Plan for Training Anyone to Witness.* Kansas City: Beacon Hill Press of Kansas City, 2002.

WAYNE ROONEY

FOOTBALL ALL-STARS

RORY CALLAN

Wayne Rooney is one
of the most talented
footballers in the world.
Read all about his
club and international
football career inside –
then flip over to find
out more about
Jermain Defoe.

EDGE
FRANKLIN
WATTS
W

LONDON·SYDNEY

First published in 2012 by
Franklin Watts
338 Euston Road
London NW1 3BH

Franklin Watts Australia
Level 17/207 Kent Street
Sydney NSW 2000

Series editor: Adrian Cole
Art director: Jonathan Hair
Design: Steve Prosser
Picture research: Diana Morris

A CIP catalogue record of this book
is available from the British Library

ISBN: 978 1 4451 0209 2

Dewey classification: 796.3'34'092

Printed in China

Franklin Watts is a division of
Hachette Children's Books,
an Hachette UK company.
www.hachette.co.uk

Acknowledgements:
Ben Angel/Action Plus/Topfoto: XIV. Matthew
Ashton/Empics/PAI: XVIII. Chris Barry/Action
Plus/Topfoto: VIII. Adam Davy/Empics/PAI:
XII. Paul Ellis/AFP/Getty Images: 18. Nigel
French/EMPICS/PAI: XIII. Getty Images: XX.
Laurence Griffiths/Getty Images: V. Mitchell
Gunn/Action Plus/Topfoto: 13. Robert
Hallam/Rex Features: VII. Andy Hooper/
Daily Mail/Rex Features: IX. Glynn Kirk/Getty
Images: 15, XVI. Tobias Kuberski /Action
Plus: 20–21. Tony Marshall/PAI: 7. Jamie
McDonald/Getty Images: 9. Jeff Mitchell /
Getty Images: 23. Peter Norton/Allsport/Getty
Images: XI. PA/PAI: 11. Nick Potts/PAI: back
cover, 5. Professional Sport/Topfoto: front cover.
Rex Features: XVII. Jurie Senekal/Getty Images:
XXI. Sipa Press/Rex Features: XXII. Mark
Thompson/Getty Images: XXIII. Neil Tingle/
Action Plus/Topfoto: 16, 19.

Every attempt has been made to clear
copyright. Should there be any inadvertent
omission please apply to the publisher for
rectification.

Note: At the time of going to press, the
statistics in this book were up to date.
However, due to the nature of sport, it is
possible that some of these may now be
out of date.

Wayne Rooney

Contents

ENGLAND'S BOY WONDER

2004 European Championships
England vs Switzerland, Portugal

It's a blazing 37°C in the Portuguese city of Coimbra. England are about to face Switzerland in their second game of the European Championships. The stadium is full – England must win this game if they are to qualify for the **quarter-finals** of the tournament. All eyes are on Wayne Rooney, an 18-year-old striker from Liverpool. The newspapers have called him "Boy Wonder".

23 minutes
England start well; their passing is good and Rooney is using his skill and power to cause the Switzerland defenders problems. After 23 minutes, Michael Owen crosses the ball into the **penalty box**. Rooney jumps and headers the ball, powering it past the goalkeeper. GOAL! Rooney runs towards the England fans to celebrate, doing a back flip on the way! The goal puts Rooney in the record books as the youngest player to have scored in the European Championships.

75 minutes
To round off an outstanding performance, Rooney scores another goal in the second half with a powerful shot from outside the box. Rooney sets up England for a well-deserved 3–0 victory.

England vs Croatia, Stadio de Luz, Lisbon

Four days later, Rooney scores another two goals – this time against Croatia. His first goal is spectacular; a blistering shot from 30 metres out sends the ball travelling into the net at 80 kph. For an 18-year-old, his power, skill and scoring ability are incredible. His 5-star performance earns him the "Man of the Match Award" and guarantees England's place in the quarter-finals.

▲ *Rooney celebrates scoring the opening goal in the match against Switzerland in 2004.*

Number one
In the space of a week, Rooney introduced himself to fans around the world as football's new superstar. Just three years before, he was sitting in school preparing for his GCSE exams – now he was England's number-one striker. *But how did he get there?*

EARLY DAYS

Wayne Rooney was born on the 24 October, 1985, in Liverpool. He grew up on the Croxteth housing estate on the north side of Liverpool City. He lived in an ordinary **council house** with his mum, dad and two younger brothers, Graeme and John. His dad had always been a devoted Everton supporter. He went to every Everton match he could get a ticket for and brought Wayne to his first Everton match when he was only 6 months old!

Everton Academy

Wayne's football talent was first noticed when he was playing with his local team in an Under-10s match. The Everton **scouts** at the game were very impressed by his skill, bravery and goal-scoring ability. As a result, they invited him to start training at the Everton Academy. As soon as he joined, the Everton **coaches** knew that they had someone special on their hands. Rooney's flair for goal scoring was obvious to everyone who saw him play. One of his Under-11 coaches wrote in his end of year report that:

"Wayne is the best natural goal scorer I've seen."

In one season, Rooney's Under-11 team played 30 games against other clubs from all over England. He scored in every match, netting 114 goals in total. In one of the games he scored nine goals!

▶ *Rooney during an England Under-15s match against Spain.*

Making the Breakthrough

Rooney made his Everton first team **debut** in August 2002 against Tottenham Hotspur at Goodison Park. He was 16 years old. However, it was his first Premiership goal against Arsenal at Goodison Park that made the whole football world sit up and take notice.

First Premiership goal

Arsenal were on an incredible unbeaten run of 30 games and were expected to steamroll over Everton. With the game at 1–1, Rooney came on as a **substitute** in the second half. He received the ball inside the Everton half and took a few steps forward. He looked around, but there was no Everton player near him to take a pass. Instead, he blasted the ball from 30 yards out towards the Arsenal goal. The ball came off the underside of the crossbar and crashed into the net, leaving Arsenal goalkeeper David Seaman with no chance of saving it.

A very special player

The goal was replayed on TV for days after and the whole country became aware of the name Wayne Rooney. The Arsenal manager, Arsene Wenger, said after the game that:

"...Rooney is the biggest English talent I've seen since I arrived in England. We were beaten by a special goal from a very special player."

▲ *Rooney in his Everton first-team tracksuit. Playing for Everton in the Premier League was a dream come true for Rooney.*

WAYNE AND MANCHESTER UNITED

After playing for England in the European Championship Finals in 2004, Rooney wanted to play in the Champions League against the best players in Europe. The Manchester United manager Sir Alex Ferguson was determined to **sign** him, and he offered Everton a massive £27 million. This made Rooney the most expensive teenage footballer in the world. Sir Alex Ferguson said:

"...we have got the best young player this country has seen in the past 30 years."

At Old Trafford

After Rooney had spent his first week at Manchester United, he knew he had made the right choice. Everything about the club was bigger and better; the training pitches, the coaches, the players and, of course, the manager. Even the subs' bench at Old Trafford had heated seats so the players didn't freeze when watching the game on a cold winter Saturday afternoon!

Hat-trick hero

Rooney made a dream debut for Manchester United in a **UEFA** Champions League match against Turkish League champions, Fenerbache. Old Trafford was packed with fans eager to see their new star signing. Wayne didn't disappoint them. He scored a **hat trick**, with two goals in the first half and a stunning free kick in the second half. United fans were delighted and Rooney was already on his way to becoming an idol at Old Trafford.

▲ *Rooney poses for the press cameras shortly after signing for Manchester United. At the time, he was the most expensive 18-year-old footballer in the world.*

THAT WINNING FEELING

For Rooney the 2007/08 season was the most successful of his career so far. His 18 goals and his creative play made him a vital part of the team. Manchester United had already won the Premier League, could they "do the double" by winning the Champions League too?

Champions League Final, 2008

In 2008, for the first time in its history, the Champions League Final was between two English clubs – Manchester United and Chelsea. It was Rooney's first Champions League Final. He said before the game that:

"...playing in the final is a great opportunity to show the world what I can do."

The first half

The Final was held in Moscow's Luzhniki Stadium. The first half was controlled by Manchester United, and they took the lead after 26 minutes when Cristiano Ronaldo scored from a header. They kept control of the game for most of the first half, but Chelsea's Frank Lampard scored an **equaliser** two minutes before half time.

The second half

The second half was tense and tough. Chelsea controlled much of the play, and nearly scored for a second time. When the whistle blew after 90 minutes, the game went to extra time. Rooney had played really well on the night, but just didn't get any clear cut goal-scoring chances.

Penalty shootout

No goals were scored in extra time, and everyone in the stadium waited nervously for the penalty shootout. Manchester United won the shootout 6–5, earning Rooney the most valuable medal in club football, and Manchester United the double.

▼ *Rooney lifts the Champions League trophy after Manchester United won a thrilling penalty shootout against Chelsea in 2008.*

Getting Better All the Time

Rooney's goal against Blackburn Rovers on the second-to-last day of the 2010/11 season won another Premier League title for Manchester United. It was Rooney's fourth Premier League medal. It earned United their 19th English League title, putting them ahead of Liverpool's long-standing record. Rooney couldn't celebrate for too long, though. Two weeks later he was playing against Barcelona in the Champions League Final.

Manchester United vs Barcelona, 2011

Rooney was looking forward to playing in front of 90,000 fans at Wembley Stadium. In the tunnel before the game, he lined up alongside Barcelona players including Messi, Xavi, Iniesta and Busquets. It reminded him that Barcelona had some of the best talent in the world on their team.

Rooney strikes back

The game started at a furious pace, but Barcelona took an early lead with a goal by Pedro. Manchester United fought back, and after 34 minutes Rooney burst forward, playing a quick one-two with Ryan Giggs. As the ball bobbled in front of him, Rooney struck it into the top left corner of the Barcelona net. GOAL! At 1–1 the game was back on!

▶ *Rooney puts pressure on Barcelona's Sergio Busquets during the Champions League final in 2011.*

Defeated by the best

In the second half Rooney knew there was everything to play for.
But Messi and Villa scored two more goals for Barcelona, giving
them a 3–1 victory. Manchester United were beaten, but there was
no shame in their defeat as they were up against what many experts
believe was the best club team ever.

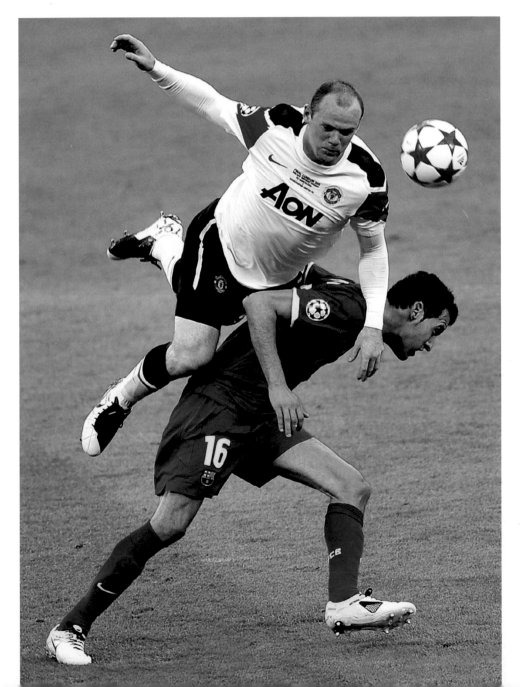

LIVING THE DREAM
– PLAYING FOR ENGLAND

Rooney was the most talented youth player in England, with an incredible goal-scoring record. He started his international career when he was picked to play with the Under-15 and Under-17 England teams. Rooney didn't get the chance to progress to the Under-19 and the Under-21 teams. At the age of 17, his ability was so good he was chosen to play for the full England team.

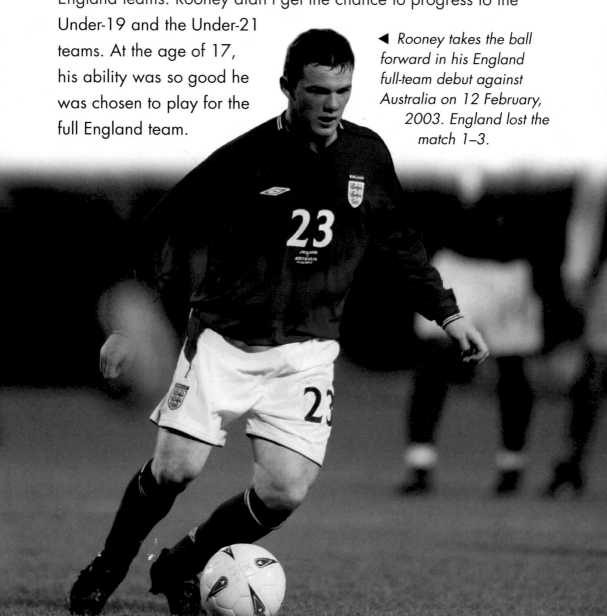

◀ Rooney takes the ball forward in his England full-team debut against Australia on 12 February, 2003. England lost the match 1–3.

Starting with the full England team

In February 2003, Rooney was called by Sven-Goran Eriksson to train with the full England squad before a friendly match against Australia. Rooney entered the record books when he came on as a substitute in the second half. At 17 years and 111 days, he became the youngest player to ever play for England. From then on he played in all the qualifying games for Euro 2004. His first goal for his country came against Macedonia in September 2003. After Theo Walcott, he is the second youngest player to have scored for England.

World Cup 2006 dreams

When he was a kid Wayne used to wear an England **replica** jersey around his estate, and pretend to be playing for his country. Never in his wildest dreams did he think that he would get all the way to the World Cup – for real!

Disaster strikes!

Rooney's preparations for the World Cup were going well when disaster struck. In one of the last games of the 2005/2006 season against Chelsea, he went down after a heavy challenge. The crowd went silent as they saw him stretchered off the pitch. The injury turned out to be quite serious – a broken bone in his foot, called the metatarsal. This broken bone would stop him playing football for at least six weeks. The news was a serious blow to England's World Cup hopes. For Rooney, it felt as if all his dreams of playing in the World Cup were falling apart.

Rooney stays focused

After a few days of feeling low, Rooney decided to do everything he could to get himself fit for the 2006 World Cup. He trained in the gym to keep in shape. Instead of running, he went swimming and cycling to keep his fitness levels up. The whole nation prayed that he would be able to play in Germany. Their prayers were answered just days before the tournament started. After a detailed **scan**, Manchester United doctors said Rooney's foot had healed and he was free to play.

▲ *Rooney arrives at hospital to have a scan on his foot. The results will decide whether he can play at the 2006 World Cup Finals.*

World Cup 2006

England finished top of their group and then went on to defeat Ecuador 1–0 in the next round. Rooney played the full 90 minutes and could feel his match sharpness coming back to him. He couldn't wait to get stuck into Portugal in the quarter-finals.

England vs Portugal, World Cup quarter finals

The match atmosphere was very tense, and there were hardly any scoring chances in the first half. Then, early in the second half, Rooney received the ball, but he was fouled by three Portugal players. As he stumbled to the ground, he stamped on one of them – Ricardo Carvahlo. The referee gave Rooney a straight red card, and he was sent off.

▲ *Rooney is shown a red card by the referee, and is sent off.*

Down to 10 men

England had to play the rest of the game with 10 men. After extra time, the game ended 0–0, and went to a penalty shootout. Unfortunately, England lost 4–1 on penalties. Perhaps, if Rooney hadn't been sent off, England might have gone on to the World Cup semi-final.

South Africa 2010

After scoring 34 goals for Manchester United during the 2009/2010 season and collecting the PFA Player of the Year Award, Rooney was ready for the 2010 World Cup in South Africa. Along with Messi, Ronaldo and Kaká, 24-year-old Rooney was expected to be one of the star players.

Twisted ankle

Then Rooney was hit by some bad luck. In a Champions League match against Bayern Munich, he twisted his ankle in the very last minute of the game. It was not a very serious injury, but it was enough for him to miss the last few games of the Premier League season.

Back in training

By the end of May the injury had cleared up and Rooney was back training with the England squad. But there was something wrong. The injury seemed to have taken the sharpness out of his game.

▶ Rooney back in action with the England squad in South Africa, 2010.

England vs USA, World Cup Finals, Group C

By the time England faced the USA on 12 June, 2010, Rooney had not played a competitive game of football for almost three months. England were expected to win the game. After the final whistle they had only managed a 1–1 draw. Rooney hadn't played well. His ankle was still weak and he was not match fit.

England vs Slovenia, World Cup Finals, Group C

Rooney put in a better performance against Slovenia in the final Group C game. He looked full of energy, and was passing and controlling the ball well. Then, with 18 minutes remaining, his right ankle began to swell up again, and he had to be substituted.

England vs Germany, World Cup Finals, knockout stage

Rooney recovered to play against Germany in the first knockout round. In an interview a week before, Rooney was asked by a German journalist if he would like to play against Germany. His reply was, ***"...of course, it would be nice to beat them!"***

Unfortunately, Germany were in brilliant form and they crushed England 4–1. After the match, Rooney was disappointed. He peeled off his sweat-soaked jersey, and stared up at the sky. He had tried his best, but with his injury, it hadn't been enough.

Looking to the future

Rooney returned to full fitness and led the way in England's campaign for the European Championships in 2012. He scored two goals in England's 3–0 win over Bulgaria in September 2011. Keep watching, because you know it won't be long before Rooney is back on the score sheet!

▲ *Rooney was exhausted after the match against Germany.*
On the day, Germany had just been too good for England.

TIMELINE GLOSSARY

Team	Appearances	Goals
League		
2002–04 Everton	67	15
2004– Manchester United	220	107
National		
2000–01 England U-15	4	2
2001–02 England U-17	12	7
2002 England U-19	1	0
2003–Sept 2011 England	71	28

Coaches People who train athletes, in this case footballers.

Council house House built and owned by the local council to rent out to local people.

Debut First appearance, in this case as a player in a particular team.

Equaliser Used to describe the goal that brings both teams to the same score.

Hat trick Three goals scored by one player in the same match.

Penalty box A marked rectangle on a football pitch, with the goal in the centre, inside which players take penalty shots.

Replica An exact copy.

Scan An ultrasound scan uses sound waves to build up a picture of living bones and soft tissue.

Scouts In this case, the people whose job it is to look out for talented players.

Sign [for] Sign a contract that commits the player to a particular team.

Subs/Substitutes Players who are ready to take over, should one of their team be injured or become tired.

UEFA Union of European Football Associations.

INDEX

TIMELINE GLOSSARY

Team	Appearances	Goals
League		
1999–2004 West Ham United	93	29
2000–2001 Bournemouth (loan)	29	18
2004–2008 Tottenham Hotspur	139	43
2008 Portsmouth (loan)	1	1
2008–2009 Portsmouth	30	14
2009– Tottenham Hotspur	64	25
National		
2001–2003 England U21	23	7
2004– England	46	15

Adrenalin A chemical (hormone) released by the body to increase the heart rate.

Caps The word used in sport to show that the player represented their national team.

Coaching Training given to athletes by coaches.

Council house House built and owned by the local council to rent out to local people.

Debut First appearance, in this case as a player in a particular team.

Dribble Travelling with the ball using a series of short kicks.

Elite Exceptionally good.

Hat-trick Three goals scored by one player in the same match.

Loan In football, a period of time spent by a footballer playing for a club that is not the club he or she is signed to, usually to gain experience.

Marker Player whose job it is to track, or "mark", a player on the opposite team.

Penalty box A marked rectangle on a football pitch, with the goal in the centre, inside which players take penalty shots.

Professional Professional football teams are made up of players for whom football is their paid job.

Substitute The player who is ready to take over, should one of the team be injured or become tired.

UEFA Union of European Football Associations.

INDEX

In an emotional interview after the game Defoe said:

"I'm lost for words, what a moment! As a young lad you dream of doing it one day. It's brilliant we've won."

European Championship qualifiers

England were eventually knocked out in the quarter-final stages by Germany, but Defoe continued his good form for England after the World Cup. In September 2010, he was once again the star as England thrashed Bulgaria 4–0 at Wembley Stadium. It was England's first qualification game for the 2012 European Championships. Defoe led the way by scoring a stunning hat trick. He was delighted after the match, telling reporters that the three goals were *"the sweetest hat trick of my career"*. He also created a bit of history by becoming the first player to score a hat trick in the new Wembley Stadium!

▼ *Defoe controls the ball in the UEFA Euro 2012 Group G qualifying match against Bulgaria.*

England vs Algeria, World Cup 2010

Defoe finally made his World Cup debut when he came on as a second half **substitute** against Algeria in England's second group game. England were under pressure from Algeria, and as a result, Defoe was denied any clear-cut chances on goal. England only managed a 0–0 draw, which left them needing to win the last group game against Slovenia to qualify for the knockout stages.

Despite the lack of goal scoring chances, Defoe worked hard, earning him a place in England's starting 11 for the next match.

England vs Slovenia, World Cup 2010

The highlight of Defoe's World Cup experience was against Slovenia in the final group game. He scored England's only goal of the match after 22 minutes; a neat volley from 6 yards out. The goal was enough for England to go through to the last 16.

◀ *Defoe celebrates with his team mates after scoring against Slovenia.*

When Defoe and his teammates landed at Tambo Airport in Johannesburg, South Africa, thousands of South Africans were there to cheer on their heroes. The England team were one of the best supported at the World Cup, because many players were familiar from Premier League games shown on TV across Africa.

Due to the high altitude, Defoe found the first few days of training tough. The team was based in a five-star luxury hotel in the city of Rustenburg, situated at 1,500 metres above sea level. At this height there is less oxygen in the air, making it difficult to breathe. After seven days though, all the players had started to adjust.

▼ *Defoe in action against Algeria at the World Cup Finals, 2010.*

SOUTH AFRICA 2010

▲ *The official England team photo showing the South Africa 2010 squad. Defoe is top left.*

For months before the World Cup, Defoe had been looking forward to playing for his country in front of a world-wide audience. As he was growing up in Beckton, he watched all of England's World Cup games with his family on TV. After each game he went on to the street to try to copy the skills of his heroes. For the first time he wouldn't be watching the games, he'd be at the centre of the action.

World Cup 2006

Slowly, Defoe established himself as a regular on the England team. His performances in the qualifying games for the 2006 World Cup were very impressive. He scored vital goals in these games, and was looking forward to going to his first World Cup in Germany. When Sven-Goran Eriksson announced his 23-man squad for the tournament, everybody expected Defoe to be included. However, in a shock move, Eriksson decided to leave out Defoe, selecting Theo Walcott of Arsenal instead.

The English public and media were baffled by the decision. Naturally, Defoe was extremely disappointed to be left out. It was a hard knock to take after looking forward for so long to playing in the World Cup.

Defoe did his best to accept the decision calmly. He didn't become bitter and angry with the England management; that wasn't his style. Instead, he worked harder than ever at his game and made a vow that he would do everything in his power to make it back on to the team. By the time the next World Cup came around in 2010, Defoe was one of the stars on the England team.

◄ *Defoe cuts inside one of Austria's defenders during a 2006 World Cup qualifier.*

England Under-21s

Defoe went on to gain 23 **caps** for the Under-21s, scoring seven goals between 2001–2003. He enjoyed playing at Under-21 level, but by now he wanted to be on the England first team. His club form with West Ham United was excellent; he finished top scorer for the club two seasons in a row. Then, in 2004, he got a call from Sven-Goran Eriksson, the England manager. He invited Defoe to train with the England first team, before a friendly match with Sweden.

England first team

Defoe was so excited when he stepped onto the England training ground. Some of the best players in the world were there, including David Beckham, Wayne Rooney, John Terry and Steven Gerrard. They looked like such fierce rivals when they played against each other with their clubs, but here they were laughing and joking like best mates!

▲ *Defoe during an England first team training session in 2004.*

XVII

ENGLAND CALLING

From an early age it looked very likely that Defoe would become a professional footballer. But would he ever make it at international level? To be picked as one of the best 11 footballers in England means you have to be an exceptional player.

Defoe devoted himself to football. He practised endlessly, followed a training routine and improved his strength. He did everything to make the most of the talent he was born with.

England Under-15 and Under-18 levels

Defoe was just 14 years old when he went to spend two years at the FA's National Sports Centre. Soon after, Defoe was picked to play for England Under-15s, and then the Under-18s. These international games gave him valuable experience. He got used to travelling and began to learn about playing against other nations.

▼ Defoe heads the ball during an England Under-21 match against Greece in 2001.

The Wigan defence began to crack, and within seven minutes Defoe scored another two goals. Most players would take it easy after scoring a **hat trick**, but Defoe wasn't finished. He continued to push forward. He was out-playing the Wigan players, and rifled in another two goals to take his total to five. When the final whistle blew, the match ended 9–1, and Defoe entered the history books as only the third man to score five goals in a league match.

UEFA Champions League

Performances like this from Defoe led to Tottenham enjoying an exciting Champions League journey during the 2010/11 season. It was his first taste of top-class European club football. He was lucky enough to be part of a team to play against Inter Milan and AC Milan at the San Siro Stadium in Italy, and Real Madrid at the world famous Bernabeu in Spain. Tottenham were eventually knocked out in the quarter-finals. But having played against some of the greatest football clubs in the world – it's no wonder that Defoe plays with a smile on his face!

◀ *Defoe celebrates with Gareth Bale, after scoring in a Champions League qualifying game in 2010.*

From the kick off, Tottenham put Wigan under pressure. They dominated possession and had shot after shot on the Wigan goal. Despite this, they were only 1–0 up at half time. But six minutes into the second half, Defoe scored his first goal of the afternoon. It was a trademark Defoe goal; he sprinted into the penalty box at just the right time to latch onto an Aaron Lennon cross. Defoe got in front of his **marker** and thumped the ball past the Wigan goalkeeper.

Tottenham Hotspur vs Wigan Athletic

On 22 November 2009, Tottenham Hotspur played host to Wigan Athletic at White Hart Lane. As usual the Tottenham players had their pre-match meal together. Defoe was relaxed; he was having a great season. He was the highest scorer in the Premier League, and was enjoying every minute of playing in front of the Tottenham fans. His confidence was very high and it seemed as if things couldn't get any better – then they did.

◄ *Defoe in his Tottenham strip in 2009.*

HIGH FIVE

Defoe moved to Tottenham for the first time in 2004, but moved to Portsmouth four years later. In 2009, Defoe was playing for Tottenham Hotspur again. He helped Tottenham to finish fourth in the Premier League in the 2009/2010 season. This meant the team qualified for the **UEFA** Champions League for the first time since 1961. Defoe was the club's leading goal scorer, with 24 goals. Without his goals, it is unlikely Tottenham would have qualified. One game in the 2009/10 season will ensure Defoe's name is remembered at the club for years to come.

▼ *Defoe playing for Portsmouth during a UEFA Cup match against Wolfsburg.*

RECORD BREAKERS

At 17, Jermain Defoe was on the verge of breaking into West Ham's first team. He had everything required to be a top-class striker in the Premier League; lightning speed, precision finishing and a unique instinct to be in the right place at the right time.

On loan at AFC Bournemouth

Harry Redknapp could see all of this in training every day. But he knew that Defoe needed to toughen up before he stepped up to the first team. With this in mind, he sent Defoe on **loan** to AFC Bournemouth. Here, he would get match practice against hardened professionals every week.

From the moment he arrived at Bournemouth, Defoe loved the atmosphere at the club. He scored on his **debut** and went on to set a new league scoring record by netting 10 goals in 10 successive games. His achievement meant that for the first time Defoe was creating headlines in the national newspapers.

Premier League debut

When Defoe returned to West Ham from his record-breaking loan spell, he was stronger, sharper and more experienced. Harry Redknapp decided that Defoe was now ready for football in the Premier League. He gave Defoe his debut at the start of the 2001/2002 season. For the next two years he was West Ham United's top scorer and became a regular in the England Under-21 team. Defoe finally left West Ham in 2004.

▶ *Defoe is tackled during an AFC Bournemouth vs Northampton Town match. Bournemouth won 3–0.*

The best coaches in England worked at Lilleshall. Their expertise, combined with Jermain's constant practice on the training ground, improved his all round game. When he arrived back at Charlton two years later he had transformed himself into a top-class player. Everyone watching him at Charlton knew that within a very short space of time he would be lining out for their first team.

West Ham United

Unfortunately for Charlton, West Ham United also had their eye on Defoe and they offered him a professional contract. Aged just 16, it was to prove the best move of Defoe's career. At the time, West Ham were managed by Harry Redknapp who recognised Defoe's talent. Redknapp encouraged Defoe to develop his physical strength in the gym and allowed him to train with the first team players. Within 18 months of signing for West Ham, Defoe scored his debut goal against Walsall in a League Cup game.

▲ *West Ham's Jermain Defoe drifts past the Chelsea goalkeeper during a FA Cup replay at Upton Park.*

Charlton Athletic

Defoe's goal-scoring instinct attracted the local **professional** clubs. He joined Charlton Athletic, and soon after he was offered a place at Lilleshall, the Football Association's (FA's) school for **elite** young players. This was the turning point in Defoe's footballing life. Every year, the FA selected 16 of the best young players in the country and gave them full-time **coaching**. At 14 years of age, Defoe was eating, training and living like a full-time athlete.

▲ A football pitch at Lilleshall National Sports Centre. The centre's facilities are the best in the country.

EASTENDER

Jermain Defoe was born in Beckton, East London on the 7 October, 1982. His mum and dad were originally from the Caribbean islands of St Lucia and Dominica. He grew up in a **council house** that he shared with his mother, Sandra and younger sister, Chonte. Defoe was raised in a close, loving family, but the area he lived in was poor. He witnessed drug dealing, joy-riding and violence throughout his youth.

Playing with passion

From an early age Defoe had a passion for football. He spent his free time playing matches on the streets and in the parks with his friends. He even went to school an hour early to have a kick around in the playground. Football was the only thing that mattered to him.

Defoe was a small boy, but even so he could control and **dribble** the ball better than most kids. Some are good at dribbling but Defoe had something extra – an incredible ability to score goals. It was this talent that made him stand out from the crowd.

School football team

When Defoe went to St Bonaventure's secondary school, he quickly made his way on to the school football team. With Defoe on board, St Bons eased their way into the Essex Schools Cup Final. To the amazement of everyone at the game, he scored six goals before half time. What made it even more impressive was the fact that he was the youngest player on the pitch.

▶ *England's Jermain Defoe during an international schoolboy match against Brazil in 1998.*

4:22 pm

England start the game with lots of energy, and they attack the Slovenia defence. Then James Milner receives the ball on the right-hand touchline. He looks up and plays a perfectly flighted ball into the **penalty box**. Defoe sprints in front of the Slovenia defender and volleys the ball into the net. GOAL! Defoe runs towards the corner flag to celebrate, his teammates jump all over him. The England fans in the stadium cheer wildly. At last, England are playing well.

▲ *Defoe celebrates scoring in the South Africa 2010 World Cup Finals.*

5:50 pm – full time

The game has ended and the scoreboard reads: England 1 – Slovenia 0. On the sideline, Fabio Capello, the England manager, looks relieved. As Defoe walks off the pitch every one of his teammates congratulates him. It doesn't get much better than this. He's playing at the World Cup and has just booked England's place in the last 16. ***But how did he get there?***

London Boy – England Hero

**England vs Slovenia – 23 June 2010,
Nelson Mandela Bay Stadium, South Africa.**

3:10 pm

Photographers and TV crews gather round the England team
bus as it pulls into the Nelson Mandela Bay Stadium. The door
opens and the England players walk swiftly to the dressing room.
Jermain Defoe strides confidently past the cameras. This afternoon
England are playing Slovenia in the final group game of the
2010 World Cup. They have to win if they are to progress to the
knockout stages.

3:25 pm – 35 minutes before kickoff

Fourteen million people are ready to watch the game live on TV.
Although the England team is packed with world-class players,
it performed poorly in the first two matches against the USA and
Algeria. Now the players must put in a top-class performance.

3:55 pm

Five minutes to kick off. The England team huddle together for
the final words of encouragement from captain Steven Gerrard.
Defoe listens to the chanting of the England fans and can feel the
buzz of the vuvuzelas sending vibrations through the stadium. His
adrenalin is starting to kick in. This is it!

Jermain Defoe
Contents

First published in 2012 by
Franklin Watts
338 Euston Road
London NW1 3BH

Franklin Watts Australia
Level 17/207 Kent Street
Sydney NSW 2000

Series editor: Adrian Cole
Art director: Jonathan Hair
Design: Steve Prosser
Picture research: Diana Morris

A CIP catalogue record of this book
is available from the British Library

ISBN: 978 1 4451 0209 2

Dewey classification: 796.3'34'092

Printed in China

Franklin Watts is a division of
Hachette Children's Books,
an Hachette UK company.
www.hachette.co.uk

EDGE **W** FRANKLIN WATTS

LONDON·SYDNEY

Jermain Defoe is one of England's best strikers – he's a goal-scoring machine! Read all about his club and international football career inside – then flip over to find out more about Wayne Rooney.

RORY CALLAN

JERMAIN DEFOE

FOOTBALL ALL-STARS

10

EVENTS
THAT CHANGED
THE WORLD

Written by Cath Senker

WAYLAND
www.waylandbooks.co.uk

First published in 2015 by Wayland
Copyright © Wayland, 2015

Editors: Julia Adams; Katie Woolley
Designer: Peter Clayman

Dewey number: 909-dc23
ISBN 978 0 7502 9127 9
Library eBook ISBN 978 0 7502 9128 6

Printed in China

10 9 8 7 6 5 4 3 2 1

Picture acknowledgements: Cover, p. 28 (bottom): © Sean Adair/Reuters/Corbis; p. 1, p. 3 (4th from left), p. 23: © David Turnley/ Corbis; p. 2 (far left), p. 7, p. 29 (top centre): © Historical Picture Archive/Corbis; p. 2 (2nd from left), p. 9: © The Gallery Collection/Corbis; p. 2 (3rd from left), p. 11: © The Gallery Collection/Corbis; p. 2 (4th from left), p. 5 (bottom left), p. 13, back cover (top left): © Corbis; p. 2 (5th from left), p. 15, p. 28 (centre, far right): © Corbis; p. 3 (far left), p. 5 (bottom right), p. 17, p. 29 (centre right): © Bettmann/Corbis; p. 3 (2nd from left), p. 19 (main image), back cover (bottom right): © Digital Art/Corbis; p. 3 (3rd from left), p. 4, p. 21, p. 29 (bottom): © Wolfgang Kumm/dpa/Corbis; p. 3 (5th from left): p. 25: © Najlah Feanny/Corbis; p. 6: © Reuters/Corbis; p. 8: © GraphicaArtis/Corbis; p. 10: © Corbis; p. 12, p. 28 (centre): © Corbis; p. 14: © Bettmann/Corbis; p. 16: © Bettmann/Corbis; p. 18: © Bettmann/Corbis; p. 19 (inset): © Monty Rakusen/cultura/Corbis; p. 20: © Bettmann/Corbis; p. 22: © Bettmann/Corbis; p. 24: © Sergei Chirikov/epa/Corbis; p. 26 (top left): © xPACiFiCA/Corbis; p. 26 (top right): © AF-Bahrain Revolution/Demotix/Corbis; p. 26 (bottom): © Historical Picture Archive/Corbis; p. 27 (top): © Corbis; p. 27 (bottom): © Corbis; p. 28 (top): © Corbis; p. 28 (centre left): © Michael Nicholson/Corbis; p. 29 (top right): © Corbis; p. 29 (top left): © Leemage/ Corbis; all images used as graphic elements: Shutterstock.

Wayland, an imprint of Hachette Children's Group
Part of Hodder & Stoughton
Carmelite House
50 Victoria Embankment
London
EC4Y 0DZ

An Hachette UK Company
www.hachette.co.uk
www.hachettechildrens.co.uk

MIX
Paper from
responsible sources
FSC® C104740

Contents

INTRODUCTION

History is full of extraordinary events that have shaped our world. Here we have chosen ten examples from the fifteenth century onwards that radically altered the lives of the people involved and those of many generations afterwards.

During the Age of Discovery from the early fifteenth century, Europeans explored the world by sea in search of new trade routes. They settled in many of the lands they found, imposing their rule on other peoples and launching an era of colonisation. European powers dominated most of the countries of Asia, Africa and the Americas until the twentieth century, when nations fought to win their independence in a series of devastating wars.

Some events marked the overthrow of a government and a dramatic shift to a new system of rule. Throughout history, revolutions have overturned the existing order and ushered in a different way of running society. The French Revolution that began in 1789 ended the feudal system under which peasants were forced to work unpaid for landowners. A few years after the Russian Revolution toppled the corrupt government of the Tsar in 1917, the Communist system developed – the government controlled the production of goods and running of services. From 1945, this system spread across eastern Europe, dividing the world between Western democracy and Soviet Communism.

Scientific developments have also changed our world. The United States of America (USA) took advantage of the invention of hugely powerful nuclear weapons to bomb Hiroshima and Nagasaki in Japan, wreaking mass destruction and ending the Second World War. Other discoveries have led to a new understanding of how the body works and advances in curing disease, such as the development of antibiotics and the decoding of DNA.

Other events triggered war: the assassination of Archduke Franz Ferdinand led to the horror of the First World War, the first truly global conflict. And Germany's invasion of Poland in 1939 was the start of the Second World War, which engulfed the world for six years.

Ten further events that have shaped our world are included on pages 26–7, and you can probably think of many more yourself!

COLUMBUS LANDS IN THE AMERICAS

On 12 October 1492, a sailor aboard the *Pinta* sighted land. Greatly excited, he alerted his captain, Christopher Columbus. Columbus was delighted to have reached India after two months' sailing from Spain. But it was not India! He had landed on what is now one of the Bahamas, the islands off the south-east coast of the USA. The local Native Americans welcomed the visitors, offering them food and water. Columbus took advantage of these peaceful people, whom he called 'Indians', and claimed possession of their island for Spain. He sailed on to take Cuba, Haiti and the Dominican Republic.

Columbus and his crew arrive in America, bearing swords.

Modern replica of Columbus's fleet set sail.

Columbus was working for the Spanish king and queen. Like other fifteenth-century European rulers, they wanted to buy spices, silk and gold from Asia. These goods were expensive because the only way to reach Asia involved a long, dangerous land journey. So they were desperate to discover a sea route to Asia. Educated people knew that the Earth was round, and Columbus thought that Asia lay about 4,800 kilometres (km) to the west of Europe. In fact, it was about 16,000 km away! Although Columbus was wrong and he had discovered America not India, the Spanish king and queen still benefited from his adventures.

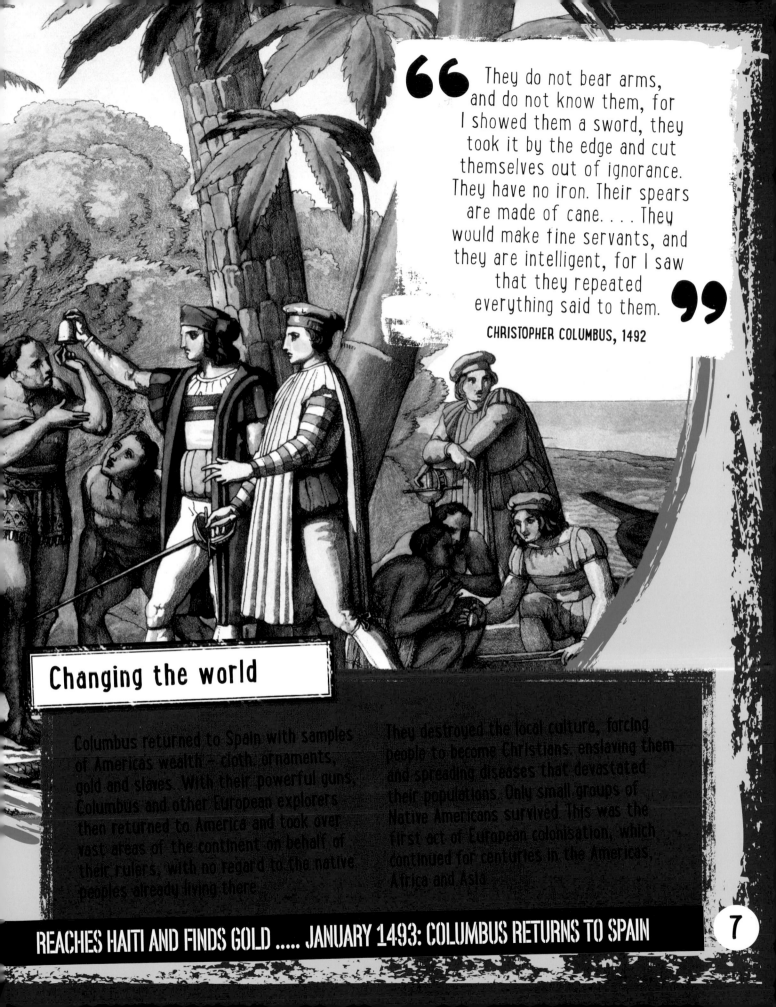

> **66** They do not bear arms, and do not know them, for I showed them a sword, they took it by the edge and cut themselves out of ignorance. They have no iron. Their spears are made of cane. . . . They would make fine servants, and they are intelligent, for I saw that they repeated everything said to them. **99**
>
> CHRISTOPHER COLUMBUS, 1492

Changing the world

Columbus returned to Spain with samples of America's wealth – cloth, ornaments, gold and slaves. With their powerful guns, Columbus and other European explorers then returned to America and took over vast areas of the continent on behalf of their rulers, with no regard to the native peoples already living there.

They destroyed the local culture, forcing people to become Christians, enslaving them and spreading diseases that devastated their populations. Only small groups of Native Americans survived. This was the first act of European colonisation, which continued for centuries in the Americas, Africa and Asia.

THE UNITED STATES DECLARES INDEPENDENCE

In the early 1770s, Britain ruled America and forced people to pay heavy taxes. The Americans even had to pay tax on the tea they drank every day. In 1773, a group of angry colonists had had enough. The protesters, some dressed up as Native Americans, boarded ships in Boston harbour and hurled all the chests of tea into the water, ruining an entire shipment.

This incident, known as the Boston Tea Party, followed a series of clashes between Britain and America. Britain had never ruled America closely – it was 8,000 km away and it took months to relay news back and forth. So the colonists usually sorted out their own problems. But in the 1760s, Britain had huge debts after fighting the French in Canada from 1754–63. To raise money, Britain decided that its American colonies should pay new taxes. Under the Stamp Act of 1765, Americans had to buy a stamp to attach to printed documents, such as newspapers. Furious traders refused, and Britain repealed the law. Britain then introduced the Townshend Act, placing taxes on goods such as tea and paper entering American ports. Again, many colonists would not pay, so Britain repealed this Act, too. However, the tax on tea remained.

The American Declaration of Independence is signed.

Britain continued to attempt to impose taxes, and the colonists grew angrier and angrier until in 1775 the tensions led to war. On 4 July 1776, after a year of fighting, representatives from the 13 British colonies of North America adopted the Declaration of Independence. It stated that the colonies were 'free and independent states', no longer ruled by Britain. But around one-third of the colonists remained loyal to Britain, and the war continued for five long years until Britain surrendered in 1781.

THE 13 COLONIES

The colonies that formed the USA were along the East Coast of America, from Connecticut in the north to South Carolina in the south. They were originally founded by English settlers during the seventeenth century.

Colonists hurl chests of tea overboard in protest at British taxes.

Changing the world

In 1783, a peace treaty was signed, recognising the United States of America as an independent nation. A government was established to make laws for the entire nation, and states set up their own governments. The loss of its valuable American colony was a huge defeat for the British Empire. Over the next 200 years, the United States greatly extended its own territory, and by the twentieth century became the most powerful country in the world, dominating trade across the globe and using military strength to maintain its position.

THE FRENCH REVOLUTION

In 1789, the crops failed in France. The French people were starving, yet their king, King Louis XVI, basked in luxury in his palace. This was normal because eighteenth-century French society was very unequal. The nobles and clergy (churchmen) were extremely wealthy and privileged but paid no taxes. The Third Estate – ordinary people – were mostly poor, but had to pay taxes to the nobles and the church.

After this crisis, the Third Estate took a stand – they formed a National Assembly (parliament) and demanded change. The king refused, so in July 1789, the Third Estate of Paris rose up in revolution and seized the government. All around France, peasants burnt down nobles' castles and took control.

Emperor Napoleon Bonaparte took charge of France at the end of the French Revolution.

The National Assembly ended the feudal system that forced peasants to work for their landlord for nothing. It introduced the Declaration of the Rights of Man, stating that all people are born free and equal. But King Louis XVI would not obey these laws. Angered by his refusal, in 1792, protesters burst into the royal palace and captured the king and queen. To the horror of all European royalty, they executed Louis the following year.

Three new leaders ruled France through a National Convention: Georges-Jacques Danton, Jean-Paul Marat and Maximilien Robespierre. But they did not rule justly. They sent spies to seek out their enemies and killed at least 17,000 people, often chopping off their heads. Despite this 'reign of terror', which ended in 1794, these new rulers hadn't been able to control France either. In 1799, a strong leader called Napoleon toppled the government, and in 1804 declared himself Napoleon I, Emperor of France. The era of upheaval was over.

JUNE 1789: NATIONAL ASSEMBLY IS FORMED ..... 14 JULY: PARIS PROTESTERS

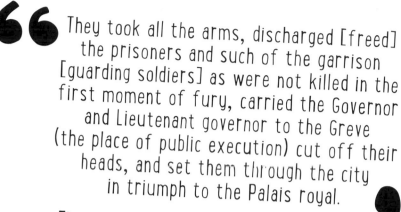

> **66** They took all the arms, discharged [freed] the prisoners and such of the garrison [guarding soldiers] as were not killed in the first moment of fury, carried the Governor and Lieutenant governor to the Greve (the place of public execution) cut off their heads, and set them through the city in triumph to the Palais royal. **99**

Thomas Jefferson, America's minister to France, witnessed the attack on the Bastille prison to seize arms on 14 July 1789

Changing the world

Although France was ruled by one strong leader once more, it did not return to the same kind of unequal society as before. Revolutionary ideas spread to other lands. In the early nineteenth century, Latin American countries fought and won their independence from Spain and Portugal. For example, in Venezuela, revolutionary leader Simón Bolívar greatly admired the French Revolution. In Europev Karl Marx and Friedrich Engels developed the ideas of Communism, drawing on the experience of the French Revolution. It inspired further uprisings, including revolutions across Europe in 1848 and the Russian Revolution of 1917.

ARCHDUKE FRANZ FERDINAND OF AUSTRIA IS ASSASSINATED

It was a beautiful summer's day on 28 June 1914, as the motorcade with Archduke Franz Ferdinand, nephew of the Emperor of Austria-Hungary, passed through the streets of Sarajevo, Bosnia. The archduke and his wife, Sophie, waved at the crowds from their open-topped limousine. At one point, the driver slowed. Assassin Gavrilo Princip rushed forward and fired two shots, fatally wounding Franz Ferdinand and Sophie.

Archduke Ferdinand and his wife touring Sarajevo, just before their assassination.

The killer was a Serb nationalist, who believed that Serbs in Bosnia should break free of Austro-Hungarian rule and govern Bosnia themselves. The furious Austro-Hungarian emperor blamed Serbia for the crime and, exactly one month later, declared war on Serbia. Both sides sought allies. Serbia joined forces with Russia, France and Britain, while Austria-Hungary was allied with Germany and Italy. Within weeks, Europe was engulfed in war.

Why did so many other countries become involved? During the nineteenth century, European countries had developed a strong sense of nationalism – they were proud of their country but often hostile towards others. Germany wanted to protect itself from any revenge attack by France, which it had defeated in the 1870–71 war. It made pacts with Austria-Hungary and Italy. France, Britain and Russia made an alliance to counter the threat from Germany's group. Now, a threat to one country meant its allies were likely to become involved, too.

Other tensions arose over empires. Britain and France ruled parts of Asia and Africa. From the late nineteenth century, Germany started to carve out its own empire in Africa, angering Britain and France. Within Europe, Austria-Hungary and Russia competed fiercely for influence in the Balkans.

FIRST WORLD WAR DEATHS

Around 9.5 million soldiers died from wounds or disease.

Around 13 million civilians died from disease, starvation or military actions.

Canadian troops, allied to Britain, charge out of their trench during the First World War, 1916.

Changing the world

The First World War lasted for four years, involved most European countries and resulted in the fall of the Austro-Hungarian, Russian, German and Ottoman empires. The mechanisation of warfare – the development of machinery to kill people on a massive scale – transformed the way wars were fought. Armies used tanks, machine guns, bomber planes, torpedoes (underwater missiles) and poison gas. The number of casualties dwarfed those of all previous wars and, unlike in earlier wars, millions of civilians were also displaced and killed.

GERMANY INVADES POLAND

It was just before dawn on 1 September 1939. With no warning or declaration of war, 1.5 million German soldiers in tanks, on horseback and on foot invaded Poland. German planes rained incendiary bombs on Polish cities. As the air-raid sirens sounded in the capital, Warsaw, citizens gazed in astonishment at the skies. They were witnessing the first demonstration of German blitzkrieg – lightning war.

The Nazi German leader Adolf Hitler was taking a gamble. He believed his forces would quickly defeat the Polish army and did not think Britain and France would challenge him. In 1938, Germany had united with Austria and seized the Sudetenland from Czechoslovakia. Most people in France and Britain accepted Germany's actions, believing German power was a useful counterforce to the Communist Soviet Union. In the same year, Hitler made the Munich Agreement with British Prime Minister Neville Chamberlain, stating that he would seize no further land.

Italian leader Benito Mussolini, Hitler, an interpreter and Chamberlain (from left) at the Munich conference, 1938.

However, in March 1939 Hitler's troops occupied the whole of Czechoslovakia and prepared to invade Poland. Realising that an attack on Poland could trigger war with its neighbour, the Soviet Union, Hitler made a surprise pact with the Soviet Union in August. They promised not to go to war against each other and secretly agreed to occupy Poland and divide it between them.

1 SEPTEMBER 1939, 04:45: GERMANY INVADES POLAND ..... 09:00: GERMANY BOMBS

> " ... all of a sudden some [Polish] soldiers appeared asking for civilian clothes to change into with the hopes that they wouldn't be captured as prisoners. They remarked, 'We are lost. Poland doesn't have the necessary weapons to protect itself. The Nazis are very well armed, motorised, with tanks and everything else.' "
>
> **Eyewitness in Polish border town Działoszyn, 1 September 1939**

German soldiers march confidently through Poland during the 1939 invasion.

Changing the world

Hitler had misjudged his enemies. When German troops invaded Poland, Britain and France declared war on Germany, starting the Second World War. In 1940, Hitler's armies swept across Europe, seizing Norway, Denmark, Belgium, the Netherlands, Luxembourg and France and imposing Nazi rule. Over the following six years, the conflict engulfed Europe, the Middle East, Asia and the Pacific, killing 40 to 50 million people – it was to be the bloodiest war in history.

ATOMIC-BOMB ATTACKS ON HIROSHIMA AND NAGASAKI

On 6 August 1945, a US bomber dropped the first atomic bomb ever used in warfare on Hiroshima in Japan. Exploding 580 metres above the ground, it created a giant mushroom cloud of smoke and fire. Around 70,000 people died instantly – many bodies simply melted in the intense heat. The explosion flattened more than 10 square km (6 miles) of Hiroshima and caused fires that burned for three days, trapping and killing thousands of people. Three days later, the USA dropped an even larger bomb on Nagasaki, instantly killing about 40,000 people and destroying one-third of the city.

The Second World War in Europe had ended back in May 1945 but the conflict in East Asia between the Allies and Japan continued. The Allies believed that an attack on Japan using regular weapons would be lengthy and cause huge casualties, while using a nuclear weapon would be so devastating that it would finish the war quickly. The US Army selected Hiroshima and Nagasaki because the first was an important military base and the second a large port. The attacks did indeed ensure Japan's defeat. On 14 August, Japan surrendered on the Allies' terms. The war was over.

A scene of total devastation after the bombing of Hiroshima.

COUNTRIES KNOWN TO HAVE NUCLEAR WEAPONS AND THE NUMBER OF NUCLEAR WARHEADS, 2014

USA: 4,804
Russia: about 1,500
France: fewer than 300
China: about 250
United Kingdom: up to 225
Israel: 75-200
Pakistan: 100-120
India: 90-110

6 AUGUST 1945: USA DROPS AN ATOMIC BOMB ON HIROSHIMA .... 9 AUGUST:

A giant mushroom cloud rises above Nagasaki as the atomic bomb strikes the city.

Changing the world

After the war, tens of thousands of Japanese people died agonising deaths from radiation sickness. Despite the evidence of mass devastation caused by nuclear weapons, the USA and the Soviet Union (which were now competing superpowers) built up their nuclear forces, arguing that they were needed for defence. Not all agreed with this approach; an international peace movement grew in the 1950s, calling for the banning of nuclear weapons. But powerful countries continued to develop them. No nuclear bomb has ever been used since Hiroshima and Nagasaki, although the USA and the Soviet Union came dangerously close to doing so during the Cuban missile crisis of 1962. As of 2014, eight countries were known to have nuclear weapons, so the world still lives with the threat of nuclear conflict.

USA BOMBS NAGASAKI ..... 14 AUGUST: JAPAN SURRENDERS

DISCOVERING THE 'SECRET OF LIFE'

28 February 1953 was one of the best days of scientist James Watson's life. He recalled, 'At lunch Francis winged in to the Eagle [a Cambridge pub] to tell everyone within hearing distance that we had found the secret of life.' Watson and fellow Cambridge University scientist Francis Crick had just discovered the structure of DNA, solving one of the main mysteries of genetics. DNA contains the genes that are passed on from parent to child, determining many features, such as eye colour, and helping to make us how we are. Crick and Watson showed that DNA is a double-helix shape and explained how it copies itself.

Crick and Watson had spent months testing out models for DNA but had not carried out any experiments to provide evidence for them. Other scientists were working on the problem, too. At King's College, London, Rosalind Franklin was undertaking lengthy and complicated work taking X-ray photos of DNA to try to discover its structure through careful analysis.

Maurice Wilkins studies a DNA model after receiving the Nobel Prize.

In December 1952, a colleague, Maurice Wilkins, secretly showed Watson Franklin's data and an X-ray photo indicating what DNA would look like if the model was correct. Wilkins knew this would have angered Franklin. The data provided Crick and Watson with vital evidence. Yet when they announced their findings, they failed to thank Franklin. Crick, Watson and Wilkins received the Nobel Prize for Science in 1962, gaining their place in scientific history. Rosalind Franklin had died in 1958, and her contribution was not acknowledged until much later.

28 FEBRUARY 1953: CRICK AND WATSON ANNOUNCE DISCOVERY OF DNA .... 25 APRIL:

An X-ray photo clearly showing the double-helix shape of DNA.

A scientist undertakes DNA research in the lab.

Changing the world

The knowledge of DNA's structure opened up a range of scientific fields, from medical treatment to food production and solving crime. In the 1970s, scientists worked out how to genetically modify micro-organisms to make human hormones and in 1978, they made insulin for people with diabetes. By 2003, scientists working on the Human Genome Project had worked out the whole sequence of human DNA. Doctors can now test people's DNA to see if they are likely to develop certain diseases, such as cancer, and researchers are developing gene replacement therapy to replace faulty genes. In agriculture, scientists have created genetically engineered foods, for example, tomatoes that do not rot quickly. Police forces can take DNA samples from suspected criminals to see if it matches DNA at the scene of a crime. The 1953 discoveries made all these breakthroughs possible.

Tearing Down the Berlin Wall

On 9 November 1989, thousands of East Germans smashed down the Berlin Wall and poured through to West Berlin to start a new life in democratic Western Europe.

Since 1949, Germany had been divided and the capital city of Berlin torn in two. West Berlin was part of West Germany, a Western democracy. East Berlin was in Communist-ruled East Germany and allied to the Soviet Union. West Germany was far wealthier than the East, with better-paid jobs and a higher standard of living. From 1939 to 1961, more than 2 million East Germans fled to the West.

One night, in August 1961, the East German government rapidly erected a wall between East and West Berlin to prevent further escapes. Once completed, the wall formed a vast concrete barrier, 3.6 metres (12 feet) high, topped with barbed wire. Armed guards surveyed the border from watchtowers and mines were buried in the ground, ready to explode and kill escapees. From 1961 to 1989, 5,000 people were caught trying to escape, and 191 lost their lives in their attempts. Nevertheless, during that time, 5,000 East Germans succeeded in crossing safely to the West.

By 1989, a democracy movement was flowing through Eastern Europe, and in October, the Communist East German government was swept from power. On 9 November, the borders between East and West Berlin were opened.

Hole in the wall: policemen examine a bomb blast probably caused by East Berlin protest groups, May 1962.

> " People helped each other; some lifted, others pulled. All along the building. people poured up the wall. At the Berlin Wall itself, which is 3 metres high, people had climbed up and were sitting astride [it]. The final slab was moved away. A stream of East Germans began to pour through. People applauded and slapped their backs. "

Andreas Ramos had driven from Denmark to witness the event

Celebrating the opening of the Berlin Wall at New Year, 1990.

Changing the world

The fall of the Berlin Wall was a significant event in the surge of democratic movements that toppled the Communist Eastern European governments of Poland, Hungary, Czechoslovakia and the Soviet Union in 1989-91. The Soviet Union split up into individual countries, which switched to Western-style market economies. While people had more freedom, a huge division developed between rich and poor in the former Communist countries.

NELSON MANDELA IS FREED

On 11 February 1990, crowds of black and white South Africans gathered outside the gates of Victor Verster Prison near Cape Town. They eagerly awaited the release of the world's most famous prisoner, 71-year-old political leader Nelson Mandela. Finally, a little after 4 pm, Mandela walked free after 27 years in jail. He and his wife, Winnie, strode through the cheering crowds, raising their fists in the air in the black freedom salute.

Nelson Mandela was a leader of the African National Congress (ANC), which opposed the apartheid system and fought for democracy. In South Africa, white people made up just one-fifth of the population but had total power and the best jobs, education, health care and public facilities available. The black majority could not vote and lived in the poorest areas in bad conditions. The government tried to crush all opposition, declaring the ANC illegal in 1960 and imprisoning many activists.

SOUTH AFRICA STATS

Percentage of black population enrolled in secondary education

1994 51%   2014 80%

Percentage of black population with access to running water

1994/5 60%   2011/12 95%

Percentage of black population with access to electricity

1994/5 50%   2012/13 86%

Mandela walks proudly out of prison to a welcoming crowd.

Children play in a desperately poor black area of Johannesburg, 1955.

During the 1970s and 1980s, the anti-apartheid campaign in South Africa and around the world grew and grew, and the country erupted in protest, strikes and violence. Eventually, the white government realised it had no choice but to lift the ban on the ANC and negotiate a peaceful settlement with its former enemies.

Changing the world

After Mandela's release, all the apartheid laws were abolished. In 1994, millions of South Africans voted in the first democratic elections; the ANC was victorious and Nelson Mandela became the country's first black president. Nations around the world that had refused to trade or play sports with South Africa in protest against apartheid now restored relations with the country. South Africa rejoined the international organisation, the United Nations (UN), in 1994. Instead of fighting with its African neighbours, South Africa now played a positive role, pushing for negotiations to end conflicts across the continent. Twenty years on, despite problems of high unemployment, crime and HIV infection, South Africa is still a democracy, and millions more people have access to education, housing, water and electricity than under apartheid.

9/11: TWIN TOWERS TERROR ATTACKS

On 11 September 2001, hijackers seized control of two commercial aircraft. Minutes later, the horrified passengers realised they were to be used as 'flying bombs', to be aimed and flown directly into the twin towers of the World Trade Center in New York. The towers burst into flames on impact, and floor by floor, they crumpled to the ground. Another hijacked plane slammed into the Pentagon, the US military headquarters in Washington, D.C.. Over 3,000 people lost their lives on that fateful day. It was the deadliest terrorist attack ever on US soil.

DEATHS IN THE ATTACKS

New York: 2,750
Pentagon: 184
Pennsylvania: 40
Emergency workers: over 400

The USA attacks Afghanistan, October 2001.

The 19 hijackers were linked to the radical Islamic group, Al-Qaeda. Fifteen of the bombers were from Saudi Arabia, the same country as Osama Bin Laden, who was widely seen as their leader. Al-Qaeda believed that the USA had too much influence over the Saudi government and was angry that US troops were stationed in Muslim Saudi Arabia. It wanted to end Western involvement in the Islamic world. Al-Qaeda turned to violent tactics to focus the world's attention on the issues and try to force change.

8:46: FIRST PLANE CRASHES INTO THE NORTH TOWER ..... 9:03AM: SECOND PLANE

> **"** You heard a big boom, it was quiet for about ten seconds. Then you could hear another one. Now I realise it was the floors starting to stack on top of each other as they were falling. It was spaced apart in the beginning, but then it got to just a tremendous roar and a rumble that I will never forget. **"**
>
> Neil Sweeting, New York paramedic

The Twin Towers collapse in smoke and flames.

Changing the world

The large-scale death and destruction wreaked by 9/11 had the opposite effect to the one Al-Qaeda had wanted. The US government became determined to increase its influence in Muslim countries and combat terrorism worldwide. It went to great lengths to root out suspected Al-Qaeda radicals and imprison them. Within weeks, the USA and Britain, with support from other Western nations, launched a military attack on Afghanistan, where they believed Al-Qaeda was based. The 'war on terror' became the main aim of US foreign policy for years to come, leading to conflicts in countries including Iraq, Pakistan and Yemen, and many thousands more deaths.

10 OTHER EVENTS THAT CHANGED THE WORLD

1. Christianity is born
In around 30 CE, the preacher Jesus was executed. His followers believed that he rose from the dead and was the Son of God, and they converted others to their faith in him. This was the beginning of Christianity, which became a major world religion.

2. The last Roman emperor falls
The Roman emperor Romulus Augustulus fell from power in 476 CE, ending the Western Roman Empire. The Roman Empire had lasted for nearly 500 years. The Eastern Roman, or Byzantine Empire, continued for another 1,000 years until 1453. Roman culture has influenced Western culture right down to the present day.

3. The Hijrah
In seventh-century Arabia, most people believed in many gods, but the prophet Muhammad from Mecca preached that there was only one God. Many people in Mecca were hostile to Muhammad, so in 622, he and his followers left for Medina to establish the Islamic faith, which spread quickly to become one of the world's main religions. Muhammad's journey became known as the Hijrah.

4. The First Crusade
The First Crusade in 1095 was the first of a series of military campaigns during which Christians travelled from Europe to the Middle East to fight the Muslim rulers for control of places such as Jerusalem, which were holy to Christians, Jews and Muslims. By 1291, the Muslims had won them back again. Tensions in the region between the three faiths still exist today.

5. The Black Death
Reaching Europe from Asia in 1348, this deadly plague killed nearly everyone affected within days. It spread across the continent and killed up to half of the population by 1350. The high death toll had a huge impact on European society.

6. Edward Jenner discovers vaccination

In 1796, English surgeon Jenner worked out that if you injected people with a weak form of a disease, they would gain immunity (protection) from a morc serious form. He developed a vaccine for the deadly disease smallpox by injecting people with the milder cowpox. Vaccination revolutionised medicine, allowing people to be protected against many life-threatening diseases, and saving millions of lives.

7. Wright Brothers' first flight

In 1903, brothers Wilbur and Orville Wright from the USA built and flew the first aeroplane with a motor. Their design formed the basis for the development of modern aircraft, which allowed people to travel further and faster than ever before.

8. The Russian Revolution

The 1917 Russian Revolution took place in two stages and ended the harsh rule of the Tsars, or emperors. In 1922, the Soviet Union was established as the world's first Communist state. The government took control of all the land, resources and production of goods. After the Second World War, Communism was imposed on Eastern Europe, leading to the Cold War between the Communist bloc and Western democracies.

9. India gains independence

In the early twentieth century, Mahatma Gandhi led a movement to demand independence from British rule. Britain finally granted it in 1947. Most other Asian and African countries achieved independence from European control over the following thirty years.

10. The Moon landing

On 21 July 1969, US astronaut Neil Armstrong was the first person to walk on the Moon. The Moon landing marked the peak of the space race between the USA and the Soviet Union. which had competed to put a man on the Moon. Since then, many manned and unmanned spacecraft have been launched into space to advance our knowledge of the universe.

TIMELINE

476
The fall of the last Roman Emperor, Romulus Augustulus, leads to the decline of the Roman Empire.

1215
In England, the Magna Carta is signed, an agreement that states that the king of England has to follow the law and gives rights to the English people.

1917
The Russian Revolution takes place in Russia, ending the rule of the Tsars and leading to a Communist government.

1914
The First World War breaks out after the assassination of Archduke Franz Ferdinand.

1939
The Second World War begins when Germany invades Poland, and Britain and France declare war on Germany.

2001
Members of a terrorist group called Al-Qaeda hijack four aeroplanes in the USA and fly two of them into the World Trade Center in New York and one at the Pentagon; a fourth one crashes in a field. About 3,000 are killed.

1492
The explorer Christopher Columbus arrives in the Americas and claims several Caribbean islands for Spain.

1776
The United States declares independence from Britain and sets up its own government.

1865
The American Civil War between the Northern and Southern states ends with the victory of the North.

1789
The French Revolution breaks out, overturning the king and queen and a republic to govern the country is set up.

1945
The USA drops atomic bombs on Hiroshima and Nagasaki, killing tens of thousands of people instantly and leading to the end of the Second World War.

1949
Communist leader Mao Zedong takes control of China and forms the People's Republic of China.

1989
The East German government is forced out of power, the borders are opened with West Germany, and the Berlin Wall between East and West Berlin is torn down.

1969
The USA lands a spacecraft on the moon: Neil Armstrong and Buzz Aldrin are the first men to walk on the moon.

GLOSSARY

abolish Formally put an end to something.

alliance An agreement between countries, for example, to work together in order to achieve something that they all want.

Allies The countries, including France and Britain, that were allies during the first and second world wars.

ally A country that has agreed to help and support another country, especially if it goes to war.

apartheid The former political system in South Africa in which only white people had full political rights and non-white people were forced to live in separate areas and use their own schools, hospitals etc.

assassination To murder an important person, especially for political reasons.

colonisation When a country takes control of another area or country, especially using force, and sends people from its country to live there – those people are called colonists.

colony A country or an area that is governed by people from another, more powerful, country.

Communism A political system in which the government controls the production of goods and the running of services.

counterforce A force that acts in opposition to another force.

democracy A political system in which all adults can vote in elections for the rulers of the country.

diabetes A medical condition in which a person's blood sugar levels can become too high.

DNA The chemical in the cells of animals and plants that carries genetic information.

emperor The ruler of an empire or a group of countries or states.

enslave To make someone into a slave, who works for their master without being paid.

execute To kill somebody, especially as a punishment for breaking the law.

feudal To do with the system where landowners owned land and peasants were allowed to work on it in return for service to their landlord.

genetics The scientific study of the ways in which different features, such as eye colour, are passed from parents to their children.

hijacker Someone who illegally seizes control of an aircraft.

HIV A virus that damages the immune system (the body's defences against disease) so that the sufferer catches diseases easily. If no treatment is given, an HIV infection causes AIDS.

hormone A chemical substance produced in the body or in a plant that encourages growth or influences how the body works.

incendiary bomb A bomb designed to cause a fire.

insulin A chemical substance produced in the body that controls the amount of sugar in the blood.

invasion When an army from one country enters another country by force to take control of it.

micro-organism A very small living thing that you can only see under a microscope.

motorcade A procession of motor vehicles.

nationalism A feeling of pride in your country, which can also mean you believe that your country is better than any other. People who believe in nationalism are called nationalists.

noble Of a high rank in society and often rich.

nuclear weapon A weapon using nuclear energy. Matter is turned into energy by splitting the nuclei, the central part of atoms. Nuclear energy is extremely powerful.

occupy To enter an area or country and take control of it, especially by force.

pact An agreement between people or countries, especially one in which they agree to help each other.

peace treaty An agreement between two hostile countries that formally ends a state of war.

peasant A farmer who owns or rents a small piece of land.

Pentagon The building near Washington, D.C. that is the headquarters of the US Department of Defence and the military leaders.

radiation Powerful and very dangerous rays that are sent out from radioactive substances, for example, from a nuclear bomb.

radical Believing in a complete political or social change of some kind, for example, radical Muslims believe in an extreme form of Islamic rule.

repeal To stop a law.

revolution An attempt, by a large number of people, to change the government of a country, especially by violent action.

superpower A country that has great military or economic power and great influence; from 1945 to 1991, the USA and the Soviet Union were the two world superpowers.

surrender In war, to admit that you have been beaten and agree to stop fighting.

terrorist A person who uses violent actions to achieve political aims.

trade route A pathway used to transport goods around the world.

FURTHER INFORMATION

Book

The Top Ten: Events That Changed the World, Anita Ganeri (Franklin Watts, 2011)

Websites

Christopher Columbus:
www.bbc.co.uk/schools/primaryhistory/famouspeople/christopher_columbus

The Declaration of Independence:
www.congressforkids.net/Independence_declaration_1.htm

The French Revolution:
www.bbc.co.uk/bitesize/ks3/history/uk_through_time/popular_protest_through_time/revision/6/

Assassination of Franz Ferdinand:
www.historyonthenet.com/ww1/assassination.htm

Germany invades Poland:
www.bbc.co.uk/history/worldwars/wwtwo/invasion_poland_01.shtml

The bombing of Hiroshima and Nagasaki:
http://history1900s.about.com/od/worldwarii/a/hiroshima.htm

Discovering the structure of DNA:
www.ducksters.com/science/biology/dna.php

Nelson Mandela:
www.bbc.co.uk/schools/primaryhistory/famouspeople/nelson_mandela/

The Twin Towers attacks:
www.bbc.co.uk/newsround/14854813

INDEX

DISCOVER MORE ABOUT WHO AND WHAT HAS CHANGED THE COURSE OF HUMAN HISTORY!

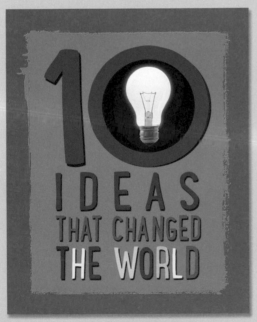

9780750291361

9780750291279

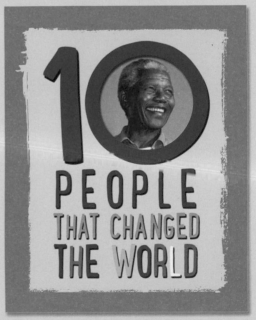

9780750291392

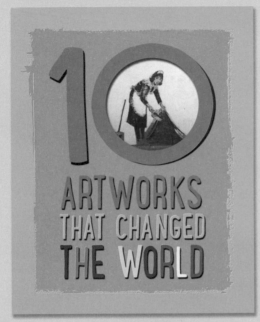

9780750291293

WAYLAND
www.waylandbooks.co.uk